Cry

A Voice in the Wilderness

Jeanita L. Sykes

Foreword of First Edition by
Apostle Naim D. Collins

Voice of Zion Ministries, Int'l
Tucker, GA

All Scriptural quotes, unless otherwise indicated, are from the Authorized King James Version of the Bible.
Some names were changed for anonymity purposes.

Published in the USA by:

Voice of Zion Ministries, Int'l
Tucker, Georgia 30085-0852

ISBN 978-0-6151-6339-0
Printed in the United States of America

Cry: A Voice in the Wilderness

"*Cry: A Voice in the Wilderness* is not just another book a person adds to their collection of literary works or uses as a coaster for beverages, but rather a testimonial and must read for any one who has ever experienced the influence, lifestyle and dominion of sin and death."

Apostle Naim D. Collins
E.S.C.A.P.E. Worldwide Ministries, Inc.
Wilmington, DE

"*Cry: A Voice in the Wilderness* is must read. This book will challenge, invoke, provoke, change and heal one holistically (mind, body, spirit and soul) ... Prophetess Jeanita has an anointing that of John the Baptist, as "a voice of one crying in the wilderness, preparing the way of the Lord, and making His path straight" (Mark 1:3) ... I recommend this book to all walks of life, cultures, institutions and ages."

Apostle Hakeem D. Collins
H.O.P.P.E Worldwide Ministries, Inc
www.myspace.com/hoppeworldwideministries

"*Cry: A Voice in the Wilderness* is more than a book; it's a Word of deliverance and healing for any one who accepts the challenge of discovering who they really are in Christ. Prophetess Jeanita Sykes knows how to capture the heart with words of strength and simplicity. I recommend this book as a road map for those who seek to break free from their past, maximize their present and revolutionize their future with principles represented in this book from this anointed woman of God."

Minister Savaslas Lofton
Columnist, Freelance Writer, and Psalmist
El Paso, Texas

"Prophetess Jeanita Sykes is one of the up and coming Prophetic Voices for this Nation and the World... when she speaks you can feel the fire of God coming out of her mouth!"

Bishop Derrick D Hunter Sr.
New Jerusalem Church of Christ
Jupiter, FL

"I have watched Prophetess Jeanita Sykes transform from a planted seed to a beautiful orchid flower. ... My sister has been called to save souls, and to show others how to progress and succeed through God's Word."

Minister Sherri Velez
Women in Christ Ministries
Atlanta, GA

- 5 -

Dedication

For Whitney, my sister in Christ
"Hasten to His Throne"

&

Father, for your gifts of Deliverance and Healing through
Christ, my precious Lord and Beloved. . .

I give praise and glory to Your Name

- 6 -

My Heart Sings Praises to the Lord: Acknowledgements

Although the project is near completion and the due thanks are finished, I want to take this time to insert a special note to a few special people.

Since the inception of this project the Lord has brought to it many wonderfully talented and anointed men and women of God. I thank our Father in Heaven for all who were instrumental in bringing this work forward.

To my dearest Apostle Naim Collins and Apostle Hakeem Collins, the one and only "Twin Prophets," praises be to our God and our Lord Yeshua ha Meshiach (Jesus the Messiah) for you and answered prayers! God saw fit that He should bless me with a double portion of love, covering, encouragement, strength, grace and power by sending you into my life. I am truly blessed and honored to have you in my life. Thank you for being midwives, fathers and brothers in the Spirit as I give birth to destiny! Words cannot express how much I love you and praise God for you two and look forward to what God is unleashing in the Earth realm for you "Sons of Thunder"! May God continue to raise you up,

mighty men of valor, as the Kingdom of God and of His Christ (Messiah) is manifested in and through you! I can hear the sound of the Spirit's rain in this season, for the thundering has been uttered!

Minister Savaslas, I praise God for your spirit of excellence and for the Lord 'setting me up' with you. Your insight has put the final touches on this work and has brought it to the level of excellence of which our God requires.

Thank you, heavenly Father, and Lord and Savior Jesus (Yeshua) the Christ! Thank You for salvation, deliverance, and for using me for Your glory! Thank You for never leaving or forsaking me, for the gifts that You have entrusted to me, and for blessing me with every spiritual blessing in the Heavenlies! Thank you for visions and dreams, for purpose and destiny!

Thanks to my mother, Phyllis Sykes, for always praying for me and believing in my deliverance for me when I could not. Thank you for encouraging me and celebrating with me the joy of freedom. For all your struggles as a single mother, and for teaching me how to endure, I praise God for you and love you.

To my brother and sister, Ramon Sykes and Mia Koehne, for your love and support and never giving up on me. Thank you Granddaddy, the late William H. Varnado, for always treating me like the apple of your eye no matter what. I miss you and love you.

To my dearest Grandmother, Lillian Varnado – thanks for not calling the police on Granddaddy when he followed you home; we grandchildren would not be here. I love you dearly for loving me as only a grandmother could. Thanks for your prayers. Praises to God for you my late Great-grandmother, Janice Jenkins-Varnado, for you praying over me as a child and teaching me to pray. God is answering your prayers. For you, Uncle Phillip, for straightening me out as a baby; and Tyree, for always loving me. To my late Aunt Josephine, for your love, making me feel special, and for ice cream!

To Phillip, my son, for all your understanding, forgiveness, courage, strength, and faith in me - I love you so dearly! For my girls, Josephine and Maria, thank you for allowing mommy the time to finish this book! You are beautiful angels!

Thank you, Marcus, for enduring all that I have put you through, for always being there for me when I need help. Thanks Doris and Sam Luckie, for being like parents to me, for forgiving and praying for me. Thank you, Sherronda Varnado, for always being there - I love you. To Nico - for forgiveness, from your favorite cousin.

Thank you, Dr. Creflo A. Dollar, of World Changers in Atlanta, Georgia, for the strong foundation in the Word. To the Honorable Pastor William McKinney of Christ Temple Baptist Church, for pastoring the Varnado family. To Dr. Bryan E. Crute, Pastor of Destiny Metropolitan Worship Church in Marietta, Georgia, for four years of prayer, for helping discover my gifts, my purpose, and how to praise the Lord and worship through living my life for His glory. Thank you, Gwen, for opening your home to me and the saints; to "uncle" Frank, for your anointing and words of encouragement; to Pastor David Owens, my "dad," for adopting me and loving me as a father I never had; to Carol Owens, for being my second mom and for your prayers! Thank you, Sherri and Olbin Velez, - I love you! Thank you for trusting me and welcoming me into your homes and hearts. Thank you for your prayers and encouragement! Sherri, thank you for your obedience. I praise God for you and for W.I.C. Enterprises and Ministry!

Finally – thank you Apostle Bala Success Abraham, for your covering and for speaking the Word of God into my life. Thanks for all your love and wisdom and fire, and to my "family" at Apostolic Triumphant Church International.

Foreword

Prophetess Jeanita L. Sykes is summoned, anointed, appointed and commissioned by the Lord Christ Jesus as a gifted revolutionary cutting-edge apostolic and prophetic voice of our time. This powerful and prolific instrument of God has been called by the Sovereignty of the Kingdom to draw her readers to the heart and mind of the Father and to impart the reality of the Kingdom of God through the Spirit of wisdom and revelation in the hearts of all humanity. She has a strong passion and conviction for the lost and in hope for a Savior. Moreover, Jeanita is endowed and graced with unique gifting to demonstrate and manifest the power of the Kingdom of God for the reason of destroying the works of darkness in and over the lives of those who are in captivity. When reading this book, you can sense the anointing and the presence of Christ as she walks you through the wilderness experiences of her life, while being captivated by the personal testimony of her victory over the powers of hell and death. Prophetess Jeanita L. Sykes possesses a Godly jealousy for men and women of all walks of life to experience the power of emancipation and freedom in the Holy Spirit from the haunts of one's past.

Likewise, this mighty woman of valor courageously and transparently carries the reader through the secrets of her life and how the love of God's own precious blood and grace translated her from the kingdom of Satan and demonic systems into the Kingdom of our Lord and His Christ. Prophetess Sykes comprehends the reality of the Kingdom and has the dispensation of grace from Christ Jesus to reveal to the world her understanding of God's influence (power) not only in her life personally, but in the Earth realm with the manifestation of signs, wonders and the miraculous. As an Apostolic and prophetic voice to the nations, Prophetess Sykes creatively shares her burden to release and deposit a Kingdom model of how the power of deliverance has wrought an indelible mark in her life outlined in this literary masterpiece.

Cry: A Voice in the Wilderness is not just another book a person adds to their collection of literary works or uses as a coaster for beverages, but rather is a testimonial and must read for any one who has ever experienced the influence, lifestyle and dominion of sin and death. In addition, this book is exclusively for those who, despite being chosen by God for a purpose and destiny to fulfill His will and mandate in the Earth, immediately find out that the enemy had another hit and assignment out on their lives to seek, kill and destroy the plan of God. Every chapter unlocks and discloses the pain, suffering, and strongholds of addictions of a survivor in the fight of her life against the tempter (Satan); she who desperately called upon the name of the Lord to save her life. Triumphantly, this artwork proves to impart and activate faith and strength in the midst of the wilderness as Jesus Christ becomes your Oasis of Eternal Life in the Kingdom of God.

I highly endorse and guarantee that after reading this book your life will be empowered and healed by the words that will illuminate your heart with deliverance and salvation, and change your life forever. God has indeed heard your cry in the wilderness!

Apostle Naim D. Collins
E.S.C.A.P.E. Worldwide Ministries, Inc.
Wilmington, DE
2007

Note from Author

Third Edition

Dear Reader,

Thank you for supporting the ministry and taking interest in my testimony. It is my sincere hope that you will be able to receive not only a glimpse into my life, but that something in my story will resonate with you. It is the express purpose of this work to reach others who suffer from some or all the same tragedies and pain that I have suffered over the years. Hopefully, my testimony will provide a hope and some key direction in your life or the life of your loved one.

Since the first publication of Cry: A Voice in the Wilderness ten years ago, I have been able to live in continued victory, grow in faith and purpose, and touch many lives. I say this so that you will be encouraged as well and know that God has a specific plan and purpose for your life (Jeremiah 29:11). This edition marks an additional 10 years of total deliverance and victory in my life, returning to school and earning both a Bachelors in Psychology and an MBA in Accounting. I have had some loss; however, all that God has done in and through me far out weight them all!

Please approach this work as more than an autobiography, but as a tool to glean valuable insight into the underlying issues that plague many today, whether a Christian or not, many will find this story relatable. Considering recent events in our nation concerning sexual misconducts, molestations, and rape, this work is as relevant as ever! As a fellow survivor of rape and physical abuse, I can testify of the Grace of God to heal, restore, and give beauty for ashes! May you and your loved ones find Him.

Cry: A Voice in the Wilderness

Contents

Introduction

This book is dedicated and written to the awesome glory of my God and Savior Jesus Christ; to all my brothers and sisters in Christ; to the broken hearted, and those who are lost and thirsting for deliverance. My prayer is that this book, which is my testimony of healing and deliverance through the Lord Jesus Christ, will serve as a tool for you to identify with, and to receive the gift of salvation and healing through the Lord Jesus. I encourage you, the reader, to not only read but also identify as possible with all the contents; looking for the similarities rather than the differences in our lives. Jesus is the same yesterday, today and forevermore. If He did for me, He can and will do for you as well by your faith.

As I pour out my heart and the heart of the Father in Heaven, I am looking to expose the works of the spiritual enemy in the lives of the people of God and those who have yet to discover that they are the remnant belonging to God. The enemy works to confuse and lie to the people of God and tell them they are not worthy and that God does not love them. This is a lie from the pit of hell! I too once believed that I was not worth God's time or love. But He soon showed me that my circumstances and struggles did not dictate who I was. Only His love for me tells me and shows me that I am who He says I am -- one redeemed of the Lord Jesus!

I urge you to trust in the Lord Jesus. Realize that it is not by accident that you are reading this book, but it is a divine appointment with the Lord Himself. He promises that if you call on Him, as I did, He will answer you

(Ps. 91:15)! One of my favorite scriptures in the Bible reads, "For in mount Zion and in Jerusalem shall be deliverance . . . and in the remnant whom the LORD shall call" (Joel 2:32, King James Version).

Also, to anyone who suffers from addiction of any sort, bondages or oppression -- know that God does not tempt us with evil nor is it His will for our lives. He may allow us to suffer, but He is not the author of our suffering. Remember Job? Though he was favored by God, the enemy tested Job with God's permission. Why? The Lord knew that Job would learn and grow from the situation. He also ordered the enemy not to take Job's life. That trial was a catapult to God's blessing Job with a double portion of all he lost! I will discuss salvation in this book as well, and pray that you will understand that your suffering is just that -- suffering and bondage. It does not mean your spiritual salvation is not being ordained and at hand, even this very day. The word says in Romans 10:9-10:

> If you confess with your mouth, "Jesus is Lord," and believe in your heart that God raised Him from the dead, you will be saved. For it is with your heart that you believe and are justified, and it is with your mouth that you confess and are saved. (New International Version)

There is a salvation of the spirit, a rebirth, which is instant and by God only. And there is the salvation of the soul - the human mind, will, and emotions - that comes with seeking and working with God; that is, working out your salvation through the renewing of the inner you by the Word of God.

Part One:

Broken Wings

- 20 -

Chapter One:
A Foundation

"Behold, I lay in Zion for a foundation a stone, a tried stone,
a precious corner stone, a sure foundation."
(Isaiah 28:16, KJV)

As a child, I had many ideas and hopes for my future - dreams of being a singer and a life full of joy and happiness. There was no reason for me to think or believe that my life would take a course of its own -- one that would take me from the innocence of a child to a life of despair, torment, and pain.

I was born in Chicago to Phyllis and James Sykes on August 16, 1969. Although my parents separated while I was still a child, my childhood years were seemingly normal; typical for the child of a single mother and sibling of an older brother, Ramon Sykes. In my early years my brother and I spent a great deal of time at our babysitter's house due to my mother's work schedule and the distance between our home with my grandparents, William and Lillian Varnado, and the sitter's home. My sitter, a surrogate mother of a sort, was the now late and beloved Doris Fletcher.

Doris is the first and lasting memory I have of an encounter with the Lord Jesus. She was sanctified and full of the Holy Ghost. She often took us to church, even at my young age of five years old. She would anoint all the children she kept with oil and prayed over us often, for sickness was never tolerated in her house! I vividly remember one night attending with her the Holiness Church she attended.

That night the church was singing and praising God with an extra vigor that I will never forget. I praised the Lord with all my heart! As it was with every night at that church, the environment was full of electricity. It felt as if I was inside a fiery furnace; yet I was not on fire. The sound of shouts of joy and triumph rang in the air as the musicians played in what seemed to be a frenzy. I could see people to my right and left with eyes closed, hands raised before the Lord in worship and adoration. As the music played and the choir lifted its voice in a wonderful harmony of praises, I began to sing and praise the Lord as well. I can not explain where a child of five years would get the kind of heartiness that I displayed; only that the Holy Ghost is responsible. I was singing unto the Lord, and remember that I began to move from side to side. After that I remember nothing except I was suddenly aware that I was at the front of the church by the choir stand. It was if I had blacked-out. Suddenly, as I stopped dancing and shouting, it felt as if the entire congregation came to me and began to exclaim the glory of the Lord on me. I did not understand what was happening at the time. I heard things like, "The Holy Ghost is on this child!" and "Praise God!" and "She is chosen by God."

It was very late by the time we arrived home. As the children were getting prepared for bed, mother Doris led me into the bathroom to wash my face. While we stood in front of the sink, she looked down to me with a deep compassion and conviction in her eyes and explained, "Tonight the Holy Spirit came on you, and you were praising the Lord and dancing and moved all over the church." She continued, "Jesus wants you!" The minute she said that, I received it. I recall feeling very special, that Jesus, God, wanted me! I felt such a sense of value and love at that moment. Little did I know that someone else wanted me as well; that there was an assignment for destruction put on my life by the spiritual enemy (the devil) of my soul. It would take me holding on to the words she spoke that night and the experience I had with the Holy Spirit to make it through some of the horrific moments that lay ahead of me.

It has come to my understanding that when God calls you, the enemy hears. Remember how at the baptism of Jesus God announced that Jesus was His Son and He was pleased. Immediately, the Spirit of the Lord led Jesus into the wilderness to be tempted by the enemy (Matt. 3:17; Luke 4:2). All throughout the history of man, this enemy has tried to hinder, kill and destroy the children of God. But praises be to our Father in Heaven; that

no weapon formed against us shall prosper (Isa. 54:17). For whom He did foreknow, He also did predestinate. Them He also called, and whom He called, them He also justified. And whom He justified, them He also glorified (Rom. 8:30).

We find in the Scripture that before David took the throne of Israel, the enemy tried to kill him through King Saul (1 Sam. 18-20). Joseph was thrown into a pit and into jail to enter Pharaoh's palace and save a nation by God's will and plan. A Pharaoh tried to kill the deliverer of Israel (Moses) as well, while he was still a baby (Exod. 1-2). And later King Herod sought the life of baby Jesus, the Messiah and King of the Jews (Matt. 1-2). The great spiritual enemy tries to ruin the plans of God.

So, it appeared that the enemy began to set in motion a lifetime of events that would attempt to derail me from the path that would lead to the fulfillment of God's mandate over my life. As a baby, there were several events and accidental poisonings that occurred in attempts to take my life, and many more accidents as an adult. But God rescued me through them all!

Growing up with a single divorced mother had many challenges, both financially and emotionally. I have no memory of my father James Sykes outside of a picture or two and a name. Often it would be only my brother and I going to church each Sunday, but nevertheless we attended. I remember walking at least four to five city blocks to church every Sunday with him and singing in the choir. I was raised a Baptist and confessed openly the Lord Jesus. I was baptized at the age of 10 or 11 at Christ Temple Baptist Church where founder and Pastor Emeritus John McKinney served as Senior Pastor. But there were already seeds of perversion, abandonment, and rejection planted for me by the enemy that would later appear in my life in attempts to destroy me.

Chapter Two:
Fatal Blows from the Enemy

"Be sober, be vigilant; because your adversary the devil, as a roaring lion, walketh about, seeking whom he may devour."
(I Peter 5:8, KJV)

Throughout the life of the person bound or oppressed by the enemy, one will always find a history of tragic events that occurred with the suffering person. A defining moment in time, which due to the event, sees a series of decisions and actions to proceed from the person, and takes him/her on a totally different path than was originally intended. There are many times a personality changes or breakdown that serves as a faulty foundation to support life for the person, leading from then on to pain, self-hatred, mistrust and debauchery. This was the case in my life.

By the time I became a teenager, the seeds, as mentioned previously, were planted by the spiritual enemy. Whether by a parent abandoning a child (the case with my father and I), or some other event that gives a feeling of rejection and abandonment, this serves as a breeding ground for the enemy to continue his treachery in promoting mistrust toward God, authorities and other people.

In my case, I did not trust men. However, I had an insatiable desire to be accepted and loved by them. This greatly affected my relationship with God as well. How could I pray to a heavenly Father while having guilt feelings? I had long felt His presence or love toward me, but I had already violated so many of His commands. The more I was disobedient toward God or my mother, or committed unspeakable perverse things, the dirtier I felt. And of course, the enemy was there to remind me just how dirty and unworthy I was.

Because of this insatiable desire to be accepted by men, I found myself always befriending boys. I grew up on the border of being a tomboy and a boy lover. All my best friends were boys. I could not relate well to girls, probably due to my feelings of their competition and fear of rejection by them. I felt I had nothing to offer them, and knew that they would see through me, being just like me; that is - a girl. I never felt I looked good enough. I would always compare myself to other girls. If I did befriend them, it was because I wanted something from them; to be more like them. Therefore, I found myself as a teen succumbing to advances, remarks and temptations from boys. I would allow myself to be put into some of the riskiest situations all in the guise of teenage experimentation and exploration.

Had it not been for the pain of trying, I would have lost my virginity at the age of 11. Fortunately, neither the boy nor I knew what we were doing. That did not discourage me, however, from still seeking the attention and companionship of boys. I found myself always having crushes on this boy or that boy. I guess to an extent this is normal for a teenage girl, but I still had an unhealthy obsession with wanting to be loved and accepted, and would go to just about any length for attention. I also often solicited negative attention from boys, but which fed my fears and insecurities even more. If I received attention from someone, that would make me feel good and I would proceed to do all I could to keep that feeling, no matter what it required.

In the summer of 1984, after my first year in High School, I was feeling quite satisfied with myself. Aside from the rebellion I had started to display in relation to my grades toward the end of the school year, I had managed to not experience any major life-threatening events. I realized, though not at the time, that I began to display a pattern of rebelling when I did not get my way, or if I believed or felt that I was not being acknowledged enough. Sadly, I would do things that would later cause me harm, but I did not realize it at the time. It was like foolishly drinking poison to punish someone.

By this time, I also slacked off in my attendance in church. My family and I had moved to the city from the suburbs and were staying in a family building on the south side of Chicago. Although I had joined my aunt's church, my heart was not into worship of the Lord. I had no idea of the true meaning of worship or dedication to the Lord. I believed, as many people do, that going to church was our duty; that this was all that was required by God. So, I simply did my duty. I would attend church on Sundays looking clean and spotless, and Monday through Saturday was my time to freely be me. I found this is one of the biggest deceptions in the Church – I thought that I was really doing God a favor by showing up on Sundays and sitting through a three-hour service. Was not that hard enough for a teen to do? So, could not God be satisfied with that difficult effort?

Now, I was aware of my sexuality. I began to develop quite nicely, and received many comments to that effect. Though I was only 14 years old, I was aware of my sexual presence and how it could affect boys. However, I did not expect, nor was I prepared for, what would happen to me that summer. It is one thing for teen girls to pretend to be older than they are, to flirt with boys. But sometimes they have no idea of the fire they are playing with – and it will burn them! I had no idea. I thought I knew what I was doing when I behaved in flirtatious manners and wore short shorts.

One afternoon there was a boy, 17 years old, whom I will call John, visiting my brother. At the time, my brother was not at home. John was listening to music and singing in my brother's room. I proceeded to enter the room and began talking to John. I commented on his singing, and I noticed a book of drawings on the bed. I lay across the bed and began looking through the book. We chatted about different things, nothing of importance. When John noticed me singing as well, he complimented me on my voice, and I ate up that compliment. I felt that he liked me. Of course, due to my predisposition to want attention, it made me feel special and pretty. In a matter of minutes, he began to talk about my physical appearance, how pretty I was, how pretty my legs were. Of course, I smiled. He touched the back of my leg and I quivered. He did not stop, and I began to feel a strange sensation, a nervousness. I wondered where all this was going to take us.

I moved his hand as he began to move it closer to my bottom, and I grew more anxious. No, I did not jump up and leave. I know that would have been the right and smart thing to do, but I liked the attention. I foolishly thought I could handle the situation and, although looking mature, I was very naïve about a lot of things as many young girls are. Therefore, the next 60 seconds or so were spent shuffling his hands from my inner thigh, to the bed, to inner thigh, and to the bed. Soon he got on top of me. At this point I panicked! Although I liked the attention, and even sought it, I did not like him on top of me. I was not willing to go "all the way." While crushing me under his weight, he began kissing my neck and saying how pretty I was. I continued squirming and trying to lift him off me; all to no avail. I cried "stop" several times, but nothing seemed to help. That day, I was definitely not a virgin any longer.

Immediately following, as I was freed, he apologized. I sat there for a minute in shock. I got up and took the hottest shower I could stand. I cannot remember how long I was in the bathroom. I remember crying for a minute or two, but not much. I felt numb. I recall that soon after I looked in the mirror and something was different. I was cold, angry, and seemingly no longer the same person. I decided that I would not talk about it or mention it ever again. I would go on and pretend that it did not happen. So, I got dressed, put on my new face, and left the house.

This event was a catalyst; an event that shifted my life into a parallel universe of sorts. No longer was I on the way to big dreams and happiness. Although many things occurred in my life by this time, this incident is the one that shattered my inner being into pieces. I could not forget what had happened. Now in conjunction with seeking the man of my life to complete me, I had to forget that I was forced to do something I did not want to do. From this point on I decided that I had to control my sexuality; use it against men. I had to be in control, but how? I took on a stronger personality type. I rebelled even more, at home and in school. I would use my sexuality to get what I wanted. I reasoned that boys (men) wanted sex. So, that is what it took to get a man, I reasoned. I also believed that if this was all they wanted, and all I had to give – I may as well use it to my advantage and not my disadvantage.

I cannot remember what I did that day after the incident. I remember feeling numb and angry. *"Why couldn't I get anyone to love me?"* I wondered. Soon however, I began my life of debauchery. I had to numb the pain. There were few things that I would not try; after all, I'm a survivor of sorts. I felt could handle anything, for what is worse than rape? Well, I will tell you. The next spirit I encountered after the sexually perverse spirit was - yes, you guessed it: addiction!

But before I delve here into the world of addiction, let us discuss some of the things leading up to my introduction to drugs and alcohol. You know what I mean -- the faces we wear to hide who we really are and what we feel and think.

Chapter Three:
The Masks

"I heard thy voice in the garden, and I was afraid, because
I was naked; and I hid myself."
(Genesis 3:10, KJV)

Often, as in my situation, we will tend to put on different faces, or masks, to hide the pain, disappointment or fear we are feeling. Remember how I have described that when I looked in the mirror something was different? I was not the same. The second mask had been put on. The first was the mask of sexuality; being a creature of beauty and temptation to get what I wanted--a man to love me. The second mask was the mask of strength. I had to be strong; after all, look at what happened! I thought, had I been strong enough, smart enough, it would not have happened. *"Weak little girl"* I thought. I felt that it was my fault. I should have been in control. I should have left the house. I should have made him stop! I went through years of hiding this tragic event from my family, my friends and myself. I did not seek professional help because that meant telling my mother, who I believed would blame me. No, I decided, I would handle this by myself.

I handled it okay, with all the know-how and wisdom of a 15-year-old girl. I began to act very tough. I kept a mean and serious look on my face most of the time. I never laughed as much as before. I began fighting and arguing, even with my beloved boys who I adored so much. I smiled when I felt pain, pretending I was okay when I was not. "How was school?" my mother would ask. I would say "Fine," with a fake smile.

The next school year was one of challenge. My grades began to decline, from being ranked 26 in a class of 839 students in my freshman year, to practically the lower percentile. I began fighting in school and acting "cool." I started smoking marijuana and cigarettes that year. That helped me to numb my pain. I felt cool and safe, and my friends seemingly liked me. I felt I finally fit in. We were misfits of sorts, but popular nonetheless. This was another mask I put on—the mask of having it all. Really, I had nothing. I was an empty shell of a person, always looking for something and never finding it. I felt miserable but could not admit it.

By that time, I also began to master my skills of self-pity and manipulation. I would have fits of rage, crying and fighting. I acted tough, talked tough, but when I wanted something I would be as sweet as my grandmother's sweet potato pie. I had also learned by that time that if men wanted me sexually, I could get things from them like clothes, money, drugs, alcohol and more. I considered myself to still be a virgin, and for months, even years, I believed it.

The summer of 1985 led to my consensual sexual encounter with a guy who was 22 or 23 years old at the time. But I began my infatuations with older men years prior. I believe that it came partially from my desire to have a father figure in my life.

Fathers - many of you fail to realize just how important it is for you to be in your children's lives, especially your daughters. A daughter's identity comes from her relationship with her father, which is the foundation for every other relationship with males she will ever have. Women who have not had healthy relationships with their fathers statistically are more prone to be abused, addicted, illegitimately pregnant, raped, disassociated, and alone. Fathers, hear this! Your children are not just a matter of financial support, but also emotional support. I would rather have seen my father regularly and had good relationship with him than any amount of money. Ask your children. You will find out what they really want and need from you—your love, attention and guidance.

Another mask I frequently wore as well was the mask of being lovable, adorable, and perfect in my ways. I pretended that I was normal, but I did not know what "normal" was. I tried diligently to strive above my shame and pain, but could not. The addition of the drinking and smoking made emotional normalcy hard to find. I soon started to experience blackouts, vomiting, and being "grounded" by my mother most of the time because of my behavior. Soon I forgot about trying to be good. I put on the mask of "I don't care" and kept going.

In many ways, although aggressive much of the time, I was what some would call passive-aggressive. I would not stand up for what I really wanted and believed. Oh sure, I could put on a good show for something that I thought everyone wanted me to want, but my true feelings were kept hidden. Half the time, I did not know what I honestly felt or thought. I was an actress, being who someone wanted me to be. This was a key trait that made me more susceptible to be seduced to do almost anything. For me it involved an inner need for acceptance. Although I fought to be strong and in control, I soon found that I was neither strong nor in control of my life.

Though I used my masks, wearing them gave me neither the advantage over others nor the security that I longed for so desperately. The masks allowed me to go deeper into deception, danger and self-destruction. The act of pretending and covering up feelings and pain only led to an elaborate web that soon entangled me for over 15 years.

Part Two:

Rebellion

- 36 -

Chapter Four:
Self-Will Run Wild

"There is a way that seemeth right unto a man, but the end
thereof are the ways of death."
(Proverbs 16:25, KJV)

Self-will run wild! That was my problem. I had resolved that I would control my life and actions at all cost. No one would control me or tell me what to do. I knew me. After all, no one knew what I had gone through or what I was feeling. How could they? I would never tell anyone my fears. I felt no one cared anyway. I was alone. I believed the Jesus I met as a child was long gone by now, and that He did not care. How could He, considering all I had done? Sadly enough, the Lord was the last thing on my mind. Now during this time, I was having too much fun, so I thought.

Throughout the remainder of high school years, I smoked marijuana and drank booze. The effect that I got from the first drink was so soothing to me; I longed to experience it again. I felt a sense of ease. The noise stopped and I was in a world of my own, one I could control. This was a place of refuge and peace for me, at least for the moment. It was easy to forget the hurt and disappointment I felt inside, and the anger and wrath I had toward not only the ones who hurt me, but at myself as well. When I was high, I could fit into any situation and dream any dream. Ironically, I found security, ease, and comfort in this life tormenting habit. It soon became my best friend–alcohol, that is. The marijuana began to make me fall to sleep and blackout on some occasions. I resolved that I would not smoke it because I was missing the party. I would go to parties, and pass out, and wake to find that the party was over. Therefore, I figured I had to leave "Maryjane" alone.

I began to stay out late with men. I would go to clubs at the age of 16 years old, dressed like a harlot. It was amazing to me that I would get past the security. I really thought I had it all. I believed that I was doing something fantastic. I was on top of the world. I had a girlfriend who was 23 years old, who would take me to clubs with her. I would stay out until morning drinking and sleeping with whomever I wanted. I felt like I was so desirable. The guys would seemingly fall all over me. This was great! This was what I had been looking for - they loved me! So, it seemed. It did not matter to me that they were just hurrying to my panties. I just loved the attention. Mix that with alcohol, and you have a winning combination I thought.

I enjoyed what I was doing. It did not matter at all to me, nor did it occur to me that I was worrying my mother to death. She would ground me, and I would do it again. Finally, it seems as
if I won the battle. She agreed to let me go out if I would beat the sun up getting home. I guess her reasoning was to compromise, or maybe she felt or realized that I would do it anyway. I am not sure. But at the time I did not care. I got what I wanted—a ticket to party! I would go to parties and barely keep my grades up. As a matter of fact, it was a miracle that I graduated on time. I transferred to night school in the last semester of my senior year at Dunbar Vocational High School and I loved my life.

Another miracle bestowed on me was that I did not get pregnant, not for lack of trying, but because of family education. I went to get birth control pills at the age of 15 and faithfully took them throughout high school. At the time, HIV and AIDS were just rearing their ugly heads up. Few had them, predominantly the gay community. So, by the grace of God I never contracted this deadly disease. Often, I wonder why, and believe that I deserved it, but God's mercies endure forever!

By the time I graduated from high school in 1987, I had had several sexual encounters, predominantly with adult men, had drunk my weight in liquor, did drugs and smoked cigarettes regularly. It appears my life, to me, was going good. I was more experienced than my peers, in my mind at least. They were immature and silly, so I thought. I attempted to go to college, but due to lack of financial means or government grants, I could not. So, I accepted that as being my lot, and kept going.

After graduation, I attempted to move to Atlanta with a cousin of mine, and make a go of life. However, due to conflict I moved back to Chicago. Shortly after, I met a man named James F. and began dating him. At first glance, I was not interested in him. However, he proceeded to take out a knot of cash and I soon caught interest. James and I dated for months before we slept together. By that time, I really grew to like his personality. I considered him to be very nice, and he gave me whatever I wanted.

And I wanted and needed it all! Because of the inadequacy that I felt always, I sought attention. The more a person gave me in attention and material things, the more valuable I felt. I began to put a price on myself, as cheap as it was. Ultimately there is no price that man can pay for a life, except another life, and there was only one who paid that—Jesus. But then Jesus was far from my consciousness. The more I delved into the life of sin that I led, the further away the reality of an Almighty God and Creator got from me.

By the summer of 1988 I needed to move to my own apartment, and he paid for it. Of course, there was a catch. He was a drug dealer and he kept his drugs at my apartment. It never bothered me in the least. He even gave me drugs to sell; although I never really sold them. I figured, why should I? After all, he paid the bills, bought my clothes, food, and gave me money. That was one thing, but I could not see myself on the corner selling drugs. That was the first time I had seen cocaine. I did not know anything about it, just that people snorted it. I tried it one time and my nose bled. I remember my mom asking me what was wrong with me, because I was hanging upside down on my bed. I said my nose was bleeding, and she never suspected a thing.

By the time I lived in my own apartment I was going to clubs every night. I had nothing else to do really. So, I slept all day, and went out at night. My mother called me a vampire on several occasions. I would often have parties or get-togethers at my apartment. I would supply drugs to my friends and they would bring drinks. I was not snorting cocaine often, only occasionally.

The freedom I felt was tremendous - though faulty and delusional. I was alone, though surrounded by many people. Fear gripped my very heart, and deep down I knew there was more, but its grasp was far from me. I believed that life owed me something; that people owed me something. I felt cheated and trapped. I figured that I could do whatever I wanted without consequences, and somehow everything would turn out right in the end after

I have some fun. I never truly thought that I had a good life, or a good childhood. I was always looking on the other side of the fence. I did not appreciate the life and safety that I was given. My mother worked hard to provide for my brother and me. She had her own struggles and battles; yet she kept us safe. I was a prisoner to my false beliefs and views on life, and I had no understanding.

Then my life of parties commenced —no rules and fun, fun, fun! I remember feeling that everyone liked me. I did not realize that they were only out to get whatever I would give them. Often times I gave money, drugs, and clothes to my friends. I was purchasing friendships and did not care. I believed that people who had surrounded me cared about me. I believed these people not only knew me but also accepted me. The problem was - who was I? What had happened to the little 5-year-old girl who was chosen by God?

Because of the choices I had made early in life in reaction to the pains of abandonment, fear, and rejection, I created a life of delusions, lies, and painful experiences. All based on self, I made choices that I believed would better my quality of life, cover over the pain and shame of my past, and make me acceptable in the sight of others. I thought nothing of my loving God and Savior Jesus. I chose to manage life myself, and control circumstances and people to be able to live in my own skin. I know how it feels to be uncomfortable in your own skin - not able to accept pain or rejection from life situations. People inadvertently hurt me at times. I never realized the impact that my destructive decisions and behavioral patterns would have on my life. The seeds that were planted began to spring up in my life. I began to see the fruit of the seeds planted. They manifested themselves in what I call character defects; that not only caused me pain, but others around me would suffer the consequences of as well.

I became at the very root self-centered, inconsiderate, and fearful of practically everything and everyone. No matter how hard I tried to gain acceptance, true love and friendship, but they eluded me. I was vengeful in many ways, very cunning, and manipulative. Only alcohol and drugs could hide the effects of my painful past. Soon I would discover that however friendly the alcohol and drugs appeared, they were the very things that would betray me ultimately and would be instrumental in my destruction.

Chapter Five:
Numb the Pain

"Mine eyes fail for thy word, saying, When wilt thou comfort me?"
(Psalm 119:82, KJV)

By the time I was 19 years old, I began to frequently hang out with a girl friend of mine from grammar school. Her name was Andrea. Andrea and I were inseparable. We spent a lot of time in school together and hung out as young adults. My mother never liked her though, and I could never figure out why. Funny as it may seem, I thought my mother was out to get me or was jealous of me. You would be surprised what goes through the mind of a teenage girl who's full of insecurities and secrets. We tend to project many things onto other people. Truthfully, I was jealous of every other girl who had a father and a mother who loved her, who went to college and was on the cheerleading team. I would often say I did not like girls like that because they were arrogant or snotty, but really, I was jealous of them and felt rejected by them. I had many delusions and paranoia going on in my teen years, and it magnified to insurmountable proportions in my adult years.

I felt comfortable with Andrea, however, because in my mind she seemed to be just like me, if not worse. Therefore, I felt safe. I believed that I had more than she had. She had already been using drugs, heavy drugs. By then she was addicted to heroine and cocaine, and needed a place to stay. I felt that I was helping, and felt a sense of superiority of sorts when she needed me. Suddenly my life was not a mess – hers was. And she needed me to help her out of her despair. Another mask I wore was one of pride and ego. Usually people who suffer from puffed up pride are quite fearful at the core; scared and feeling inadequate. I can say so confidently because I was one of them.

Being quite skillful at managing my usage of drugs and alcohol, I felt that I could handle just about anything. However, I was experiencing at the time rejection from James. He had a girlfriend and I knew it. Oftentimes I was hardly able to see him. I was in love, so I thought, and I wanted him for myself. Although he took care of me, I wanted him with me consistently. We would sleep together only once every two or three months. But that opened the door for me to see other guys. After all, I felt, who did he think he was rationing out sex? I was in control, not him! But it seemed he was trying to control me! I could not have that! *"I will show him"* I thought. So, I slept with other guys. I did not care about them much. I just wanted sex and more money.

James was quite proud of the fact that I did not, so he thought, use cocaine. Although I snorted cocaine from time to time, I never smoked it, which was then called "freebase" or "smoking." At times James would rant and rave about it to his family; how I was a "good girl" and so on. Therefore, when I had taken all I was going to take in rejection from him, I decided that I would crush and embarrass him by smoking cocaine.

Of course, Andrea, who at the time smoked cocaine, knew all about it and was all too willing to show me how to do it. She considered that I would be an endless supply of it. So, I tried it. I remember having such a rush. It was quick, yet exhilarating, unlike anything I had ever experienced before. I wanted more! From that point on I tried to recapture the first feeling I had in trying it, but it became more and more elusive to me. Each time that feeling of ease and comfort got further and further away – *there it is … almost got it … no not quite … gone. Let's try again.* This cycle of feeling is what is meant by, "One is too many and a thousand not enough." And this went on for about a week.

Then Andrea and I began to argue about the drugs, and we decided not to do them anymore. We threw everything away and vowed never to do it again! That devotion lasted all of two weeks or so. Then the thought occurred - *"Well, let's try it again. If we argue we'll stop. It won't come between us."* However, it did - repeatedly. Andrea began to steal from me, and I would put her out of my house. She would come back, we would make up, and do it again. This became the cycle with us.

Soon James discovered something was wrong. Drugs were missing, and I was out of sorts. He stopped bringing or giving me drugs to sell or keep, and I started scheming on how to get more of them. I would lie and cheat to get them – whatever it took! By that time, I was not paying my rent because I would buy drugs with the money. Eventually I got evicted.

In the meantime, I had met a man named Russell, who I had done business with previously. He liked me, so I depended on him to get me an apartment on South Shore Drive. We began seeing each other, even though he was 38 years old and I was 19. He had two daughters, one of whom was almost my age, and I spent a lot of time with him. For a very short time I stopped using drugs. However, when Andrea came around, I would use again. I am not blaming her for my choice to use; she was just influential in my decision. My mother would always say that whoever introduced me to drugs was not my friend. Andrea showed me how to use drugs, but I made the decision to do them. In addition, I had already been addicted to alcohol and had snorted cocaine occasionally. I admit I found it true that if you stay around people who use drugs, chances are good so will you.

For months, I stayed at Russell's house, while having an apartment around the corner from there. I played housewife. I cooked, cleaned and hung with his girls. I felt a sense of security. I finally had a place where I belonged, where I was valued, so I thought. I could not, however, shake the habit of cocaine. I would snort it often and smoke it only on occasion. Finally, I hooked up with some folks in my building, and did it almost daily. By then James was back in my life and I had a drug supply again. So, I bounced back and forth from my house to Russell's. I was not sleeping with James then.

Soon James left me again and I continued with Russell. But Russell hung out in the streets a lot, and I became angry and felt neglected. Who is he, I felt, to leave me here with his children? I am not their mother! So, I left and moved to my apartment, and continued my using and drinking. But soon I discovered that I was pregnant by Russell. I decided to not tell him and have an abortion.

Of course, I did not stop using drugs; yet I decided not to abort my baby. I was still very small in size for pregnancy, and being evicted now again. My belongings were put out on the street, and I went to stay with a friend. I lost all my belongings; yet I did not care. I just wanted to get high. Russell did not know about the baby I was carrying, and I was too delusional and selfish to see what was happening to me. My life had taken a terrible turn -- several of them! I just could not grasp the gravity of my situation. I was in total denial. I did not tell anyone I was pregnant except Andrea, and I told her because she was pregnant too.

- 47 -

Soon I would discover that this was only the beginning of my troubles; although it seemed that maybe the baby I was having would serve to be the inspiration I needed to get my life together. After all, now I had another life depending on me! Not only that, I would finally have someone who *really* loved me, no matter what may come our way! Things seemed to be looking up, or at least I had new hope for a future.

Chapter Six:
Calm before the Storm

"For he that waverth is like a wave of the sea driven with the
wind and tossed."
(James 1:6, KJV)

A calm rest before the storm. At this juncture in my life, I sought

peace - but there was no peace. In writing this chapter, it did not occur to

me until later that it was the shortest chapter in this book. With good

reason, it seems out of balance, for my life was out of balance. It is no

coincidence that it is short, because the semblance of peace I experienced

during this time was in fact just as brief as this chapter.

Shortly after staying with a friend, my grandfather came to visit and

beseeched me to come home. He saw that I was a hot mess. Agreeing to

return to the safety of my grandparents' home, I packed what little clothing I

had and left with him. No one knew now that I was with child, and I

welcomed the break from using drugs and painful reality. I was also

experiencing nightmares; that is, a recurring nightmare. This giant furry and

purple monster was chasing me. Wherever I ran, although I would feel safe

for a moment, it would inevitably find me and come after me. It took me

years to figure out the meaning of this dream that was tormenting me. I

discovered its connotation a little over five years ago, and I will divulge its

meaning later in this book.

My family decided that I should return to Atlanta and stay with my

cousin. Although my mother knew what was going on with my addiction, the solution given to my dilemma was to relocate. *"The problem was definitely my environment"* I thought. So off I went once again to Atlanta. This time, my cousin and I managed to get along together. I found a job in a chicken restaurant and proceeded on with my new life with my baby. The drug use was finally over! I did not even drink! Things seemed to be going well even though no one knew I was pregnant.

One day my cousin Sherronda said, "Those pants make you look pregnant." I said, "I am." She was in shock and very angry that I did not tell her about my pregnancy sooner. She soon got over it and urged me to write to Russell and tell him; so, I did. I never heard back from him.

I continued to work up until my son Phillip was born. I remember how little his face and hair - so pretty. He was a good baby. However, my cousin and I had another disagreement and I moved back home. This time it would be different. I had somewhat of a year without drugs. *"I'm okay"* I thought to myself, *"The past is over."* I stayed with my mother for a month or so before she helped me get an apartment. My brother moved in with me to help, and things seemed to be going okay.

Upon my return from Atlanta, I went by Russell's house to show him the baby. He had a new girlfriend and half way paid attention to Phillip. Many said that Phillip looked just like him. He did, and does to this day. I could never understand why Russell would not embrace him. I was totally pissed at Russell! I hated him for rejecting us! I never called him again until years later. I decided that I would take care of my baby myself. I did not need Russell! He was only doing what all men do - leave!

I enjoyed my apartment on the south side of Chicago. I stayed in a lower-class neighborhood than did my grandparents and mother, but I was content with my surroundings. So-called "bad neighborhoods" are not so bad when you live there. You tend to get to know the people that scare so many others, and it becomes part of your life. You become part with them. So, it seemed I was on my way in the joys of motherhood, and making a life for my baby and me. Things were okay for a while there. I managed to be there a couple years in all. However, before I left I was plunged back into the life that I thought I had escaped.

Chapter Seven:
The Downward Spiral

"And sin, when it is finished, bringeth forth death."
(James 1:15, KJV)

Living on the south side of Chicago was going well. My mother had moved to the suburbs, so I rarely saw her. I did not visit my grandparents either due to distance. For a while, my brother was the only family I saw frequently. Later, after my brother moved out, I started occupying my time with the neighbors. Yet again, my inability to see the gigantic "hole in the street" allowed me to rush in as only a fool would do. I had no idea of the dangers that lay ahead and waiting. I was totally oblivious that these new so-called friends would play an intricate part in an elaborate scheme to keep me in darkness and chains. Only in retrospect do I now see the traps that were laid in my life to detour me into a life of destruction - a decision here, an incident there - all carefully orchestrating my path.

It is strange how you can meet someone for the first time, and not know that this person is going to influence your destiny in such a way that, had you known it, you would have run as fast as you could in the other direction. Oh, how many of those moments, chance meetings, relationships, and events I would long to now change. Nevertheless, I now see that I had to experience these things. I had to meet these people; otherwise, I would not be here today. All part of the law of causality, you see, one event that causes a reaction or another event to happen. Where would I be now?

Certainly not writing this book. Certainly not possessing my three beautiful children. Once again, I am reminded that God does order our steps, and that truly "all things work together for good to them that love God, to them who are the called according to His purpose" (Rom. 8:28, cf. KJV).

I met my neighbors a few months after moving into my apartment, and only spoke occasionally when we passed. I soon discovered, however, that something was going on over there that caught my interest. I soon sensed the behavior of drug use (funny how an addict can find drugs anywhere anytime). We have a keen eye for seeking out money, sex and drugs. Soon I became part of the local clique. I would use and drink regularly with them, and soon discovered that the neighbors upstairs from me used drugs as well. It did not take long for my home to become a revolving door for men and drug users. I continued to allow drugs around my child without any regard to his or my safety.

But soon I had to move again. Only this time nothing was thrown on the street. I moved in with a guy I met, who appeared to love me. He gave me an engagement ring – that I later found was fake -- and we rented the home across the street from his parents. The house was okay because I was happy to not be on the streets with my baby. Soon, however, I discovered that we were not the only residents. "Mickey" and his family were also taking up residence. I woke up one night to see two of the biggest rats I ever saw in my life, running across the counter in the kitchen! This greatly disturbed me, but I had no where to go. I prayed that one of those nasty rodents would not bite me or my baby. I stopped cooking and eating at home, and never ventured aside from my bedroom, the bathroom and out the door!

A month later, I was awakened to a deranged woman outside screaming my guy's name and threatening to break all the windows! I told him he better go outside immediately and speak with her. I discovered that day, not only did he propose with a fake ring, but he should not have proposed at all - he was still married! He just decided to leave home one day without notifying her. In addition, his family knew this and never said a word. So that morning I left him and moved in with a friend. I lived with her about a year or so. We got along well considering. However, this was not the end but the beginning of my downward slide.

Soon after leaving him, the married guy continued to try to contact me, but I would not give him another chance. He had lied to me. I did not appreciate being involved in adultery without my knowledge. Granted, adultery did not bother me since I did it often enough. I just wanted to know when I committed it. I was very self-righteous, you know. I had my morals and all to live up to. It is funny, the web we weave for ourselves, the lie and delusion that we buy into. For years I thought I was out-slicking everyone when I was out-slicked, out-foxed by my addiction. My addictive lifestyle seemed normal to me.

At my new location, I began to hit the streets again. I had a babysitter when I wanted, but often my girlfriend would go out with me. I saw James again a few times, though never seriously. He would give me money if I needed it. I will never forget the disappointment I saw on his face when he saw me. I felt like a disgrace, but would cover it up with a well-to-do attitude. I started smoking cocaine again, and snorting and drinking as much as I could stand. Many times, the cocaine would take over and I rarely thought about my first love - alcohol.

During this time, I also met another man who I got pregnant by. But I felt he was definitely "bad news" and so I had my first abortion. It made me really depressed at the time. I did not like the idea, but I felt no good choice in the matter. Besides, what would I possibly do with two kids? I could not take good care of one, and I was seriously trying to get away from the father. He had me doing all sorts of things I did not want to do. That was my ticket away from him. We traveled a lot, and I felt pretty much like a hostage to him. He kept close eye on me, and when I went home for the abortion, I never returned to him.

After the abortion, once again I decided to go back to Atlanta. My life was mostly "not" working out in Chicago. I needed a change of pace and environment. So, my brother and I returned to Atlanta. Before leaving, I took my son by his grandparents to see Russell once again. Phillip was two at the time and that is the last time either of us ever saw Russell. Oddly though he spent time with Phillip. His attitude seemed to have changed. However, after further years of attempts, I was unable to contact or locate him ever again.

My brother and I shared an apartment, and things were okay. I found a job and was working, and his fiancé would babysit Phillip for me. Things were good on the outside, but not on the inside. There was still a void and sense of fear that I could not shake. I was still experiencing the nightmare on occasion and was very disturbed. Soon after arriving in Atlanta, I ran into John again. Yes, my perpetrator in the flesh. Oddly enough, years had gone by and, although I was still angry deep down, I could not admit it. I did not even think about it. Too much time had passed and too many drugs. As sick as this makes me feel -- I looked at him not as someone who harmed me, but as someone who loved me and needed me.

I began to consent to sex with John, although I felt guilty about it and ashamed; it was as if I could not help it. Soon my brother returned to Chicago and I was left alone in Atlanta. After staying with another cousin for a couple of months, I finally got a place of my own. I had been drug free now for about a year. I was working as a temporary employee for several different companies and finally I was at a dry time. No work was found for me. It was November of 1993 and I had no money. I had recently met my daughter's father, Marcus. I remember walking to the store and he was there staring at me. I asked him what was his problem, and could I help him, and it was history from there.

Marcus told me about strip clubs; that a girl can make a lot of money dancing, and I would probably do well. Although I had a son, no one would be able to tell. I went to the club and spoke with someone, and they suggested my coming to amateur night. I did and won! Of course, I had to be drunk to do it, but I did it! This really gave me a sense of power and control sexually. I enjoyed having power over men, having them longing for me and having desires for me. I absolutely enjoyed the money. My son had a wonderful Christmas! I bought him everything -- video games, clothes, toys, etc. I bought a car as well, and I could pay my bills.

In addition, Marcus was living with me, and that was even more income. Although our relationship was rocky at times and we fought, we did have some good times in the beginning. I do admit that I took him through a lot, and was a major part of the problem. I evoked jealousy and mistrust in him and was very rebellious and combative as well. Although that is my part in it, it was not the only part. He had a part as well in the fighting and our unhappiness. However, I am not writing to blame anyone, only to tell what happened in my life, and how the Lord saw me through it.

I would arrive home drunk after working, and soon began staying out even later than the clubs are open. The year and a half I had clean was gone. I began using cocaine again. It was not long that I began smoking again. Although not as often as before, I used again, and again, and thought I was controlling my usage. Slowly, the fighting increased. It was a vicious cycle: I would use, Marcus would get angry, and we would fight, and that would prompt me to use even more. This in turn, prompted him to argue and fight even more. I did not know what to do outside of medicating myself to numb all my emotions and fears. We would break up and make up. This went on for years.

I experienced only very brief intervals of clean time from drugs, to be followed by even longer bouts with drugs. This was a cycle of mine for over 11 continuous years. During my career as a stripper, I had managed to get pregnant three times, had two additional abortions, and a miscarriage. I remember the day I stopped stripping. It was truly a divine moment. I was sitting at the bar in the club I worked in and began to look at the people around me in a most peculiar manner. I began thinking *"I don't know these people. I'm revealing myself to strangers."* I looked on stage and noticed the girl dancing and singing to a song by a popular rock band that blasphemed Jesus! Suddenly, I heard someone next to me - although I sat alone, say *"Child of God, what are you doing?"* I immediately thought to myself, *"What am I doing?"*

I proceeded to the stage and waited for the girl to finish her set. When she approached me, I asked her, "What were you saying?" She said, "huh?" I continued, "What was the song you were singing, you know…" and I began to hum the melody. She could not look me in the eye. I thought it strange enough that she was singing an anti-Christ song, but I wondered why she could not look me in the eye.

It was not me that asked her what she proclaimed but the Holy Spirit. During my clean time, I had joined a church in Atlanta that taught me about the Holy Spirit. I had received the baptism of the Holy Spirit with the gift of speaking in tongues. That night, I walked into the club office and quit and never returned to dancing again. One down and several bondages to go. I left and enrolled in school. I returned to church, as I had several times ago, but yet again. But I was not finished with my battle against drugs and alcohol.

Once again I made a firm resolution to never use drugs again. I was a new woman! After all - I am a child of God, the head, not the tail. Amazingly, I had to learn that when we give our lives to Christ, it is a total submission of our will to His. It takes our faith and trust in the Lord that He be our all-in-all. I discovered that I only thought that I was allowing Him to be Lord of my life. I still had secrets. I still carried the shame of my past and my sins, and I still carried the spirit of addiction with me everywhere I went. I was still selfish at the core and fearful. It would still take a much deeper plunge into darkness and despair for me to totally surrender my life to the Lord.

Part Three:

Denial is not a River in Egypt

- 62 -

Chapter Eight:
Fig Leaves

"And the eyes of them both were opened, and they knew that they were naked; and they sewed fig leaves together, and made themselves aprons."
(Genesis 3:7, KJV)

By the time I was nearing the end of my academic endeavor, I was getting quite irritable. There was no valid reason; things were seemingly going quite well. I had almost a 4.0 grade point average. I was state President of a business fraternity and Student Government President. I had met the Governor of Georgia, Zell Miller, and won state wide competitions. I should have been happy, but unfortunately, for the addict that is not enough. I was still feeling inadequate and fearful of success. For the addict, he/she would find a reason to use just because the sun is shining.

I found more masks to put on, had sewn together fig leaves to cover my nakedness, and deep down I knew I was going to fall—and hard. I always had this feeling of impending doom that I could never shake. Fear gripped my very soul in every area of my life. I thank God that I did not completely lose my mind. I was an absolute mess. Shortly before graduation I was in a car accident and broke my leg. This caused me to be very depressed and angry. After all, it was not my fault; yet I was maimed. It was a long road to rehabilitation but I managed to recover. Soon afterwards I began to use drugs again. Slowly at first, once every so often, then it began to interfere with school and work. But I managed to graduate and return to work. Soon I received a settlement, not nearly as much as I should have, but

I accepted it out of wanting something. I had already started using again and this was a lot of money. So I bought new furniture, clothes, a computer, gifts for friends, and used drugs. I remember thinking to myself, *"I'll just spend $40 dollars then stop."* I never could stop there, and it would go on all night. I began to be late for work and Marcus and I fought more and more.

I tried everything I could to hide my using, my shame. It baffled me how Marcus could always tell when I was high. It also irritated me to no end. Who was he to tell me what to do? My favorite saying was, "I'm grown and I do what I want." I also remember just how deeply my disease of addiction deceived me. I always thought that I could stop whenever I wanted to. I did not have a problem; I just used drugs and sometimes it got out of hand, but I could stop if I wanted. I just had a little habit, that is all. It never dawned on me at the time that I did try to stop, and could. The problem was staying stopped! Now that was the kicker! I never realized it at that time, as clear as it was to everyone around me. I would continuously minimize my using and drinking. We are always the last to admit our wrong. Do we really think it normal to use drugs every day? Or run in and out of treatment centers and jails? To constantly become homeless? Strange as it seems, I thought that was normal. I did not see any of the insanity of my life.

For years I would hide, using in the bathroom, other peoples' homes, in my car while driving. I was desperate for another hit of cocaine. I remember clearly one day riding down the street. I was looking for some more drugs and was very high. I remember wanting to stop, but I was on automatic. I cried out at that moment to God and begged Him to help me, to deliver me from all my pain. I thought at the time that He might instantly part the skies, take His hand and pick me up, and brush me off, and set me in happy-go-lucky land.

I was totally clueless to the requirements I had to meet for Him to help me. Many do not like to hear that, but it is true. There are a required mindset and decisions we must make to work with God on our deliverance. Healing is a process. Yes, God can and has healed some instantly, but for some of us it takes a process of God revealing Himself to us to get us into total deliverance and victory. It is a deep work, and it is a complete work, if done with honesty and willingness.

The medical community classifies alcoholism and drug addiction as disease. For some diseases, there are typically no cures, only a prescribed remedy for relief from the symptoms. Also, substance addiction is the only disease that makes you believe you do not have it. How elusive and cunning is that? Only the spiritual enemy can be behind this one! Now here is where 12-Step programs meet Christianity. Jesus came to set the captive free! Free I say, not into further bondage. But for now, I will not explore this point. My main objective is to help you the reader to reach a point of clarity to enter the process of healing and deliverance from the bondage of addiction. Believe it or not, there is a balance that must be attained for the real addict and alcoholic to achieve sobriety. The deeper issues come later, much later for some than others, but our heavenly Father is a loving and patient Father who does not give up on us.

He did not give up on me. In fact, He had already determined when and how I would come out of this despair I was experiencing. Unknown to me at the time, I had another five years of suffering to go. Why? Well, I was not ready for healing yet. I had not had enough. I needed to learn more.

Remember, God did not bring this on me; however, He allowed it. He allowed it because He already knew I would come through at an appointed time. Also, it is no coincidence that "5" represents the number of God's grace. It is five years now, almost to the day, from the time I surrendered to God and the day I began this book. Jesus fed the multitude with two fish, and five loaves of bread. David slew Goliath with five smooth stones. And a couple of years ago I found that the root of my first name is the same as the Apostle John's, and it means "God is gracious." The Word says, "[He is] declaring the end from the beginning" (Isa. 46:10, KJV). This is enough proof to be convinced that not only have I been predestined to be here today writing to you, but you are also predestined to be reading this, and to be conformed into the image of His Unique Son.

Chapter Nine:
The Pink Elephant

"For sin, taking occasion by the commandment, deceived me,
and by it slew me."
(Romans 7:11, KJV)

Let us take a moment to talk about the family and friends of the person in bondage. Much like my family and friends, I am sure that you can relate to not quite knowing what to say or do about your loved one, or yourself if you are suffering. Perhaps your family or you choose not to discuss the problem. In doing this we can think that the problem will somehow lose its power over us if we do not talk about it. After all, talking about it gives the problem validity and life.

The "pink elephant" is that subject or problem that everyone in the room knows about and can see, but pretends is not there. It is obvious—it is pink and weighs a ton, and is in the middle of the living room! We can hardly fit into the room because it is so big and loud! Why is it pink anyway? Odd color for an elephant. Oh well, just walk around it, pay it no mind; he will eventually leave – soon we hope. Whether it is drugs or alcohol abuse, or sexual abuse in our families, or an affair, or a divorce, we can all identify with this element of denial.

No one really wants to admit when there is a problem in the family. Too often it becomes a reflection on our character as it relates to the person. Perhaps some feel they may be to blame. Whatever the reason, this is one of the major obstacles in the way of a person who is suffering. Whether it comes from an overly protective mother, or sibling, a spouse who wants to protect children, or from ourselves, we must get past this major admission hurdle if we are to experience true freedom.

No one knows about this pink elephant more than me. For years I walked around, past, under and over this metaphoric creature. In the beginning of my bout with addiction, many of my friends and family were aware of the constant using I was engaging in, the lifestyle I had chosen. Few would discuss it, especially with outsiders. Only when I began to display outward signs of my addiction, affecting my health and the well being of my children, did I begin to hear regular pleas of concern. I, even considering my obvious failures, was not willing to admit or accept that I had a problem. In my perception, it really was not as bad as they were suggesting. So, I knocked back a few, or spent my entire paycheck on drugs. I managed most times to work it all out. The truth was I was sinking fast. I had spent a great deal of time trying to control my using and drinking. The consequences were insurmountable
and the wreckage was piling up. It became harder and more stressful to put out the fires, construct lies, and obtain my drugs. Slowly but surely, I began to sink into a deep depression, and this prompted more using. I did not see any way out of my nightmare. Sadly enough, at the time I was not looking for a way out. I had long since given up on the dream of having anything close to what resembles a normal life.

As I approached the end of my struggle with addiction, the elephant began to get bigger and larger than life. There was hardly any room for me in the same room. I could no longer deny what was staring me straight in the eyes. I had a problem—a huge problem! What happened? How had I made such a mess of my life? As I asked these questions, I still engaged in using. There was nothing I could do about it. The urges were too strong. I had no defense against the drug and the alcohol monkey.

In the spring of 2000, I had reached an all-time low. I was once again being forced to move out of my apartment on the southwest side of Atlanta. I knew that it would happen. I was up all night smoking crack, trying to escape the inevitable. Once started, I could not stop. I knew I had to pack and move, but I was totally enthralled in the drugs. Suddenly a knock came at the door, it was the movers. I had to hurriedly grab belongings, purse, and pack whatever I could. The rest was wrapped in sheets and put out. Luckily, my daughter's father came to help and moved my furniture and things into a storage unit. The mind of a normal person; that is a non-addict, would have seen this as a sign of an underlying problem. To the addict it was a minor inconvenience, that is all, nothing more.

I stayed in a hotel, still wanting to use more drugs. I was in total denial as to what was really going on. I minimized the situation as much as possible. Marcus constantly tried to reason with me, and of course I put on the tears. I cried and pleaded with him and my mother. I needed help! I did not know where to go or what to do. My mother had been telling me for years, "You need to go to a meeting." By this she meant a 12-Step recovery meeting. I had long since convinced myself that I was not an alcoholic or an addict, that I could stop when I wanted to. If I went to a program, that would be like admitting defeat. Somehow, I related going into treatment with the derelicts I saw on the street corners that picked through garbage and slept on park benches. I was not that! No way! I will not go there!

Now, however I had nowhere else to go. So reluctantly I went to a treatment facility. While there I could meet some other people, who appeared to have been going through what I was going through. It seemed that I was finally in a safe place. I would beat this addiction thing, and get my life back on track.

While in treatment I discovered that I was an addict and alcoholic. Amazingly, it was not the doctors or therapist that told me. I discovered it myself by looking at my life and the lives of people who had already admitted to being alcoholics and addicts. The similarities were staggering. It was much like listening to someone else telling your story. It gave me a sense of relief to know that I was not alone. And they seemed to care about me as well. I felt had not experienced someone caring for me and not wanting anything in return. This also amazed me. While in treatment I began to understand, with prayer, the dream that I was having that consisted of me being chased by the huge purple monster. I realized that the monster represented the part of me that was an addict, and no matter where I ran, or how hard I tried, I would always be found by him. There was no time to rest or enjoy life. He would always be coming over the horizon. As I embraced my addiction, the dream stopped. After having this same dream for over a decade, it suddenly stopped, and I have not had that dream again since that year.

It would be wonderful to tell you that this was the beginning of a wonderful journey down the road of happy destiny. That everything was beautiful and I got my life back at this point. It would be great to tell you that I left treatment, met the man of my dreams, got married, and live in a two-story brick house with a white picket fence. As much as I wanted such as that to be the case, it is in fact only a dream that I had at that time. Rather I would have more to learn about addiction, the Lord, and myself.

- 73 -

Part Four:

Divine Intervention

- 74 -

Cry: A Voice in the Wilderness

Chapter Ten:
Falling Apart

"For I know that in me (that is, in my flesh) dwelleth no good thing: for to
will is present with me; but *how* to perform that
which is good I find not."
(Romans 7:18, KJV)

While in treatment I learned a great deal about addiction and my actions. However, there was nothing proceeding from the lessons, therapy groups, or my mentors that could teach me what I have come to know and understand as the key to my progressing in recovery from my addiction. Although I had a great desire to become free from my suffering; that is, the consequences of my actions, it would not be enough to propel me into a deep and rigorous work of "housecleaning" and submission to God. Neither would my desire to save my family and my job serve as a good motivation and fuel to move forward in faith through the process of deliverance that I so wanted and longed for.

I was admitted into a residential program and attended meetings and group sessions regularly. I found someone who was willing to help me through the process, along with other women and counselors who supported me. Unknown to me, I had what many refer to as a "lurking reservation." Deep within me I thought that someday I would be able to drink alcohol and manage using again. On special occasions, perhaps I could drink some wine or something. I was focused on getting out of the treatment center and getting back to my job and children. I had also met a man in a meeting, who

I was sure was the answer to my problems. He understood me and I understood him. We were perfect together - so it seemed. So, I proceeded to balance my recovery with my relationship with him.

It did not matter much to me that he was still legally married to one woman and living with another. He had professed to love *me*, not them. The warning signs were all there, sure enough, but I had long since trained myself to ignore anything close to a conscience. I continued to see this man, and began focusing on fixing our relationship. Manipulation and control were my key attributes and tools that I would use to bring about my happy ending that I so desired. Unfortunately, I would learn much too late that I am not the director of life, God is. However, I still attempted to force God to accept my will as opposed to me accepting His. The Bible says that there is a way that seems right to man, but the end is destruction. It took me a few months to learn this lesson.

After a couple of failed attempts of sobriety, I managed to get pregnant and have another abortion. It really broke my heart to do it. I really wanted my baby and thought that I was in love with this guy. I am not using his name for personal reasons--involving another life that is not my own. Shortly after the abortion I left the residential program. I felt that I knew what was best for me after all. Those people did not know me, and I believed that they did not even like me. Since then I have found that they are one of the few groups of people that I would ever meet that would not judge me, and would love me for me, and truly want me to recover from addiction. The mind of the addict is unlike any other. We as addicts are egotistical, paranoid, and think we know everything. We have constructed a web of lies that encompasses our lives and identities. We as addicts have faulty belief systems, self-righteous judgments and resentments that, when left unaddressed, can ultimately ruin us.

Upon moving into my own apartment, I continued to use drugs again. I stopped going to any of the support groups or meetings, and proceeded to live my life as I saw fit. Because of my continued relationship with the man I had met, I conceived again. This time, I refused to abort my baby. Although I was using I had resolved to have my child, and I informed him of the news. He never knew about my using again; I hid it from him as best I could. He in turn accepted my decision as best he could at the time. Eventually I stopped all contact with him.

So here I am, pregnant and in full-blown addiction. I tried my best to stop. I knew what I was doing to my baby, but was powerless to stop. I spent many nights crying out to God to help me, with seemingly no answer. I joined a church and remember specifically having prayer one day. The church pastor prophesied and said to me: "The Lord said, that what the devil meant for bad in your life, He is going to turn around and use for good." Somehow, at that moment I knew that God was going to help me and save me from my despair.

If you are reading these words and are struggling with addiction or any sort of bondage, the Lord says to you -- "What the devil meant for bad, to destroy you, I am going to use it for My glory." Know, dear one, that the Lord has heard your cries of anguish from His Holy Mountain, and there is healing and deliverance available to you this very day!

A few weeks after the prophecy, I was in my room. I was using crack and in terrible pain and torment. I remember the pain of that day and praying to God, once again, to remove the taste of the drugs from me. I remember specifically concluding that this was my life. I resigned to the fact that I was an addict and that I would always use drugs and never be free; that this was my lot in life. I felt I would ultimately die in my addiction. This was a lie from the spirit enemy, but at the time I did not know it. He was trying to kill me—destroy my testimony and me. But there is One greater than he that is in the world. The greater One's name is Yeshua (Jesus), and He has come to set the captive free!

One day I called the church pastor's wife. I began to share with her my struggle and ask for help. She counseled me and prophesied, although I do not think she knew it at the time. She said: "If you don't stop what you are doing, you will lose your children and possibly go to jail." I knew that something bad would happen; yet with all the will I could muster, I just could not stop. I would go a few days at the most, but the desire and craving to use would always win. I found myself thinking to myself, *"I'll just do one and then stop, just to get the edge off."* But one would lead to one more, and one more would lead to all night. It was a vicious cycle that seemed to never end.

I was on my way home from work, September 27, 2001. I was eight months pregnant then, and had decided that I would get a small amount to use that day. I arrived home with drug in hand and proceeded to use. Although I had been experiencing some discomfort that day, I had dismissed it as normal pregnancy issues. As I took the first "hit" I began to experience more pain. I knew something was happening to my baby. *"Oh God,"* I thought, *"let her be okay!"* I called Marcus and told him what was happening, and he came immediately. The thought occurred to me that something may be very wrong with her because I had used my entire pregnancy. But I dismissed that -- no time to think of that now – she is coming! It was a very quick labor! There was no time for an epidural. I had her naturally, and she came quickly! I remember praying that she would be healthy; that I had not damaged her permanently.

By the time she arrived, I learned that she was healthy; that is, she had ten fingers, ten toes, and so on. She was beautiful! I was ecstatic to know that finally -- she was here and seemingly healthy! It was a quiet night. But I rested as best I could with the thought and feeling of some impending doom lurking within my soul. I wondered if they would test her for drugs. I prayed that nothing would show up, part of my delusion no doubt. How could I hope that nothing would show up when I was using just prior to labor? The insanity of my life was paramount!

The next day, which was a Friday, two women came to see me. They proceeded to tell me that my baby was born with cocaine in her system. My heart dropped. My world came crashing down around me. They continued to tell me that they would keep her in the hospital until child protective services came, and that I would have to appear in court before a judge to answer to charges. I cried! I could not believe what was happening! How I could have done this to my baby, to myself and my family! I was out of control and powerless to help my situation or myself. I sank to an all-time low. I cried all day! I was embarrassed and ashamed at what I had done! How would I tell my mother? My son? I cried some more. I felt like the ultimate failure! I knew I had let everyone down, including God. *"I deserve to die,"* I thought.

That next Monday I went to court. As the judge handed a sentence, I remember thinking that my life was over. He said that all my children were to be put in the protective custody of the department of children and family services. I would have to enter a treatment program, be monitored for usage of drugs, and have home visits by the department regularly. I would be allowed only supervised visits with my children. But by the grace of God I was not sentenced to jail time. However, no jail could compare to the "prison" that I had built for myself. I asked that my oldest daughter be allowed to stay with her father, Marcus, since he was active in her life more than I at the time. The court allowed that; they gave him temporary custody of Josie. I believed that this would minimize her trauma. I could not bear the pain of her being placed in a strange home at such a young age. She would not understand -- she was only two years old then.

However, to Phillip, my beloved son, I would have to explain the events. I would have to tell him that his mother was an addict and that she had used drugs while pregnant with his baby sister, Maria. How ashamed felt, but I had to get home to explain it to him before they took him. I rushed home as quickly as I could!

Chapter Eleven:
Pain is a Great Motivator

"But we glory in tribulations also: knowing that tribulation worketh patience; and patience, experience; and experience, hope."
(Romans 5:3-4, KJV)

Arriving home, I noticed a truck parked in my driveway. The man sent to retrieve my son had already arrived. I rushed into the house. I hugged Phillip as tightly as I could. He was 11 years old then, and he was confused and scared. I explained to him, "Mommy has made a great mistake. She did a very bad thing." I continued to explain all that had happened. I told him that I was sick; that I had a problem and needed help. I concluded with, "I will get you and your sisters back," and, "I will get help and we will be together again," and, "I promise." The man took my son, and I was left alone.

I sat on the sofa, crying from the depths of my soul. I looked on the wall at the pictures of my children and cried. I recall the feeling of being ripped from the inside out -- a feeling that surpasses the pain of death of a loved one. I felt naked, alone, afraid, and hopeless. I cried from my heart and soul to God for help. I was tired of the pain and struggle, and needed and longed for a touch from my heavenly Father. Suddenly I heard a voice say: "Go back, you know what to do." And that I did. I remembered that there were people like me, people who were addicts and alcoholics, who somehow had overcome their addictions and were living free and happy. I suddenly knew that if I went back to the meetings I had once half-heartedly attended, and gave it my all and trusted God, then I would be free.

All I wanted was for the pain to stop. I felt so alone and ashamed. The only thing I knew to do at the time was to go to 12 Step meetings and ask someone for help. There was no church group that I knew of at the time that could help me. I thought to myself, *"The last time I asked for help from the church, I was told simply to stop, but I couldn't."* It was as if they did not understand. I had nowhere else to turn except the group of people who had experienced what I was going through. After finding a treatment program, I began a rigorous routine of attending meetings, group therapy and visiting with my children. Phillip was in a group home, and Maria was put into the home of a woman named Sherri Velez.

The struggle to recover was not an easy one, but I believe that because of the pain I experienced, the grace of God and encouragement, and the help from others, helped to give me the willingness and courage it took to continue. There were several lapses, however, in my attempt to accumulate consecutive days of sobriety. Maria was born in September of 2001. My sobriety date is November of 2001. It was very difficult in the beginning to fight the mental obsessions and urges to use. I remember the day I totally surrendered to the process of recovering from my addiction. I had used, and was on my way to get some more drugs. If you are an addict, you will understand what I am saying. As I was on my way, I had what could be called a moment of clarity -- the light bulb finally came on! I realized that if I get one more, I will get another and another, and it would never stop and I would lose my kids forever. Suddenly I knew that I could not do just one—not ever! I realized the key was never to do the first drink or drug. Wow! What a concept! That is what they were talking about when they said, "One is too many and a thousand is not enough."

That night I surrendered and never looked back. I set my mind to do all I could do, all that was required of me, to recover. I would get my life back, my children, and be free from the grips of alcohol and drugs once and for all! I set out on an honest and rigorous program of recovery. I would do everything that I was told. I would not pick up, no matter what! I was told that if I had the urge to use, to call someone and get to a meeting. And this I did. I remember the first time I experienced this miracle. I was on my way home and suddenly, out of nowhere, I thought, *"I'll just go get one, no one will ever know, and I'll go on about my way."* Then I remembered: the one will turn into two, then three and so on. I picked up my cell phone. I called everyone I could and proceeded to go to a meeting. After speaking with several people who were also in recovery, my desire to use left. I experienced the miracle! Each time the urge came, I did what was suggested and it worked; it got easier and easier. Soon, as I continued to do the work required to recover, the thought and desire to use left me. I began to believe that maybe this would work, there was hope for me; that with God's help through this program I was in I could and would recover.

During this process God could heal my heart of the pain and hurt I had suffered throughout the years. Unforgiveness was a part of the prison I had built for myself, and it was a key foundation to the lie that I was living. I had much resentment towards my family, John, James, Andrea, my children's fathers, and numerous others. My bitterness had locked me into a curse of pain, despondency, poverty, and loneliness. Only through a deep, honest desire, hard work, and prayer, was I able to be set free. Not only did God use conventional means to administer healing to me, but He also used intensive prayer and intercession by pastors and deliverance ministers. The desire to use drugs and alcohol has been removed by God. My recovery will be five years now, as of this November 2006, and the Lord is continuously transforming me by His Spirit.

- 85 -

Part Five:

God's Plan for Salvation

- 86 -

Chapter Twelve:
The Message

"And they overcame him by the blood of the Lamb,
and by the word of their testimony."
(Revelation 12:11, KJV)

I want to take a moment to clarify a couple things. As mentioned in Revelation, we do overcome not only by the blood of Jesus, but by the word of our testimony. This is what the enemy has been after my entire life and yours, our testimony of Christ. What has the Lord done for you? You see, beloved, it is in our testimony that every word is established; that others hear the gospel of Christ; that they receive hope and deliverance. In the Gospels, we see where Jesus' reputation preceded Him. Many had already heard of the Son of David who had fed thousands and healed the sick; therefore, when He came to their town, they were expecting a miracle from Him. In fact, many sent for Him, like Martha and Mary.

It is not easy for me to share all my testimony with you. But for the glory of God in Christ I share with you, the reader, all that God has done for me, that you may be made whole. You see, as I said in the beginning, we should always look for similarities. It is in the similarities that you will see that if He did for me, He can and will do for you.

There is no problem, no addiction, or affliction to big for Him. This is a message not only for the lost, but for all who are in Christ as well. How many of you are singing in choir, teaching Sunday School, working in ministry of any sort; yet there is a secret something that is looming over your head, your very soul. The enemy is in your ear, reminding you how unworthy you are, that you are a hypocrite, you are not saved, you are going to die; that you better not tell anyone, if you do they will judge you and kick you out of the church – "You know you shouldn't be sleeping with her," or, "He's married and you're a jezebel." You see, these are lies and bondages from the enemy, and God has promised deliverance from them all. Those bondages are no different than drug addiction. Drug addiction and sexual addiction are similar in the eyes of God.

That is where I was missing truth. I thought that somehow, because I was addicted to drugs, that I was not equal in the eyes of God to someone who was not addicted. I also thought that somehow there was a difference between a murderer and a liar. How wrong I was! Sin is sin. If we are guilty of one sin, then we are guilty of all, says the Lord. However, I also discounted the redemptive work of the Cross. Jesus already died for my sins, for sin and all unrighteousness (1 John 1:7-9). My trials were not because I was a bad person, or undeserving of God's love. Rather, as the Lord said to the disciples in the instance of the man born blind, "but that the works of God should be made manifest in him" (John 9:3).

In addition, though I give the above analogy to help with identification of our need for deliverance, I need to make one thing clear -- all our sins have been forgiven. Romans 10:9 states, "If thou shalt confess with thy mouth the Lord Jesus, and shalt believe in thine heart that God hath raised Him from the dead, thou shalt be saved." That is it! We are saved by faith, and faith alone. None is righteous, says the word of God. If we could do it by our acts, then the Lord would not have needed to come and die on the cross for us.

How does this fit into the life of the person who is currently bound by the oppression of some sort of habitual sin or addiction? First the Word says that, "Let no man say when he is tempted, I am tempted of God: for God cannot be tempted with evil, neither tempteth he any man: But every man is tempted, when he is drawn away of his own lust, and enticed" (Jam. 1:13-14). What does this say? Well first, temptation does not come from God. When Eve was tempted in the Garden, it did not come from God, but from the enemy. Also, Eve was led away by her desire and lust to be like God. The book of James goes on to say in verse 15 that, "When lust hath conceived, it bringeth forth sin: and sin, when it is finished, bringeth forth death." Adam and Eve died a spiritual death that day, and every man born of Adam is born in sin and spiritual death, cut off from God. God's plan for the fallen state of man is in Christ Jesus, He who knew no sin, but became accursed for us. Isaiah says, "He is despised and rejected of men; a man of sorrows, and acquainted with grief: … we esteemed him not. … yet we did esteem him stricken, smitten of God, and afflicted. But he was wounded for our transgressions, he was bruised for our iniquities: the chastisement of our peace was upon him; and with his stripes we are healed" (Isa. 53:3-5).

Job's faith was tried by the enemy. It was the enemy who wanted to try Job; of course, he had to ask God's permission, because Job belonged to God. This is something we must understand beloved. We must understand that if we are in Christ, then we belong to God and nothing - I mean absolutely nothing - can happen to us unless God allows it. We must also remember that God did not give the devil power to take Job's life. Out of all the circumstances and consequences I experienced because of my rebellion and trial, the enemy could not take my life. I praise God for that, if nothing else. God did not give up on me! He already knew that He planned an escape. Paul writes, "Who shall separate us from the love of Christ? Shall tribulation, or distress, or persecution, or famine, or nakedness, or peril, or sword? … For I am persuaded, that neither death, nor life, nor angels, nor principalities, nor powers, … shall be able to separate us from the love of God, which is in Christ Jesus our Lord" (Rom. 8:35-39).

I would also like to state that God uses people to help us and to heal us. Yes, God has delivered people instantly from bondages and afflictions. I am a firm believer in and living testimony to His miraculous and instantaneous powers. However, there is a process of healing that some of us must go through to achieve total deliverance at the level and depth that God intends for us. All knowledge and wisdom comes from God. Just as we would go to a doctor if we were in a car accident, God has established doctors, therapists, and processes that we can go through to experience healing.

One of the barriers that I had to get over was the barrier of a 'know-it-all' attitude. You see, I thought that I knew God. I believed that there was nothing that a 12-Step program could tell me about God; after all, I was raised in church. It never occurred to me that I only thought I knew God. Upon studying the history and founders of the very first 12-Step program, I found that God inspired the program. The original intent of the program was to show men and women how to have a relationship with God; yes, the God of Abraham our father, and to become free from the grips of alcoholism and addiction. Of course, some will argue this fact and men through the years have applied their own interpretation of the original intent of the founders, but nevertheless the program works. One should also know that every other 12-Step program has sprung from the original one that was founded over 65 years ago. In addition, this program originated with a religious group, The Oxford Group out of Ohio, and its steps and principles adopted by the co-founders of Alcoholics Anonymous. The principles taught by 12-Step programs are all Biblical in nature and origin. I am a strong advocate of programs of this nature. Why? "All things work together for good to them that love God, to them who are the called according to His purpose" (Rom. 8:28). I have been called according to His purpose, and so have you!

Today more and more churches are either allowing 12-Step organizations to use their facilities, or they are implementing their own program of recovery for the community and the members. If you are one who suffers from any addiction, or you know someone who is, I encourage you to contact your local church or hospital to get more information about recovery programs in your area. Keep in mind however, that Christ centered programs are my suggestion, for it was Christ alone that saved me. A Christ centered program helps us to discover the deep level of love that God has for us, and our need for forgiveness and reconciliation to our Creator through Christ. It is very important that you hear the gospel and understand that Christ is the Son of God, and that through Him alone will we obtain everlasting life and forgiveness of sins. It is also as equally important that your life be saved today, that you get help for your problem immediately. I trust that God will reveal His Son to you today.

I give God all the glory for my deliverance from drugs. I understand that it is only by the blood of Jesus that I am here today to tell you what He has done for me. It was the Lord who delivered me, not me, not man, but the Lord Himself. In the coming pages, I will show you what the Word of God says about His promise of salvation and deliverance. I will show you how the Lord, working through prayer, people, and His Word, has brought me to where I am today.

Chapter Thirteen:
A Promise

"Before I formed thee in the belly I knew thee; and before thou camest forth … I sanctified thee, and I ordained thee a prophet unto the nations." (Jeremiah 1:5, KJV)

Soon after embarking on my journey to recovery, I began to experience the hand of God visibly acting on my behalf. On several occasions, I began to hear His voice, see miracles happen, and see answers to prayers. I was learning how to accept God's will for my life, as opposed to forcing my will on Him and others. I began to pray and trust Him daily for my well being, as well as for a defense against using. It was miraculous to me, to see that months had gone by and I had not used or drunk any alcohol. By the time I had 90 days clean, I got Maria and Phillip back. I was elated! Maria was beautiful, and had displayed no visible or medical signs of damage of any sort. That was the most precious miracle -- my baby was healthy and normal. I attended meetings every day and worked with a woman who had committed to help me to work through the process of recovering. As we went through our text, the first promise was that I would recover -- it was on the page, in writing. How amazing it was to me that someone was guaranteeing that I would recover if I did exactly what he or she did. It was much like a recipe. If you do what they did, you would get what they got -- freedom from the desire to use and drink.

At six months clean I attended a conference for recovering addicts. It was astonishing to see so many people who had suffered from the same pain that I had. I found out early that I was not the only woman who had used drugs while pregnant or that had lost her children. What a relief it was to know that someone related to me, that I was not alone like I had previously believed. While attending, I found that there were men and women who had been sober for 40 or more years! Wow! Who would have thought that this could happen? I never conceived of anyone being sober that long. I wanted what they had. They were happy, free from fear, and loved one another, no strings attached!

On the last day, there was a count down from the most years in sobriety to the one with one day clean. To see a stadium full of recovered addicts standing one by one, who had years, then months, then days clean was breath taking! As I looked at the thousands around me standing, I heard a voice, the same voice I had heard before, and He said, "You will never have to use again." As tears flowed down my face, I knew that I was finally free, that the deliverance that I prayed for years ago was here.

You see, I had resigned my life. I believed that I had to use, and that this was the life I was dealt. Just as some are born wealthy or poor, I thought I was born and made to be an addict. That was what addicts do - they get high. What a lie. The Lord Himself spoke and said that I did not need to; just as if He had said, "Woman, thou art loosed from thine infirmity" (Luke 13:12). There was birthed in me a new hope, a new assurance, not in myself as I had trusted before, or in men, but in the Lord Jesus. He was here, He was working everything out, and I would be free and whole. I decided that I would work even harder as I prayed and sought the face of the Lord.

For months, I attended meetings and worked with other women who helped me tremendously. I had many who encouraged me as I walked down the road of recovery. Surprisingly enough, Sherri, the woman who kept Maria in foster care, became a friend. From the first day, I met her she welcomed me and prayed for me. She told me that she knew that I would get Maria back, and that God loved me and was with me. She saw His presence on me, she would exclaim. What an encouragement she was in that period of my life! It is very important and paramount to have a group of people and believers who can encourage us and pray for us and stand with us. There were many others as well who I cannot mention by name, but you know who you are.

During a season of seeking the Lord, I would read the Word, listen to tapes from friends, and watch broadcasts of select preachers. God led me into a fast and prayer time where He began to reveal even more to me. Beloved, we are delivered and saved only that we may glorify the Son and our Father in Heaven. "This sickness is not unto death, but for the glory of God, that the Son of God might be glorified thereby" (John 11:4). This is His will, that all look unto Christ, and that all things come under Christ to the glory of God.

One night I was listening to a message by Bishop Eddie Long of New Birth Cathedral in Georgia. The message was entitled "Push through the Pain." A friend had loaned me the tape and burned it to a CD for me. As I was fasting the Lord led me to listen to this message, and I did. I played it all night every night of the fast. One night the Spirit of God came on me. He literally lifted me from my bed and put me on my feet! I began to pray, as the Spirit gave utterance. He would release me to sleep - I would drift off

- then He would wake me again, put me on my knees, and I would pray some more. This went on three or four times throughout the night. At that point, I heard the Lord say, "Go to the brook where you will be fed, bring an offering unto the Lord, and cleave unto your husband." I also heard, "Be the voice calling in the wilderness."

That morning, although I was praying all night, I was refreshed - as if I slept eight hours. I remembered the Word and promises of the Lord. I then began to search for the brook, but where, I thought. I loved Bishop Long, and still do, but it was so far from me. Sherri called a couple days later and invited me to go to a church she visited, and it was around the corner from me. As we arrived I immediately fell in love. The praise was wonderful! The love of the saints, and the Word was powerful yet simple and easy to understand. That was the day I was introduced to Destiny Metropolitan Worship Church. I still wanted to go to New Birth, but I could never arrange it. Apparently, it was not God's plan.

The next service I attended at Destiny I will never forget. Dr. Bryan Crute, Senior Pastor, was teaching on the five-fold ministry, and gave the acronym W-F-E-D-M (Worship, Fellowship, Evangelism, Discipleship, and Ministry). "We feed 'em," he said. Immediately my spirit jumped and leaped, and I knew this was the place! I joined that day and began to learn and grow by leaps and bounds in the Lord! Here I learned also that as the Lord spoke to Jeremiah the prophet, to speak unto the captives from Jerusalem, He has spoken to me and to you. "For I know the thoughts that I think toward you, … thoughts of peace, and not of evil, to give you an expected end" (Jer. 29:11).

Beloved, did you hear that? Through all the captivity of addiction and trials and hurts, the Lord has thoughts of peace and good, and most of all an expected end. This said to me that He was not in the least surprised about what I was going through. He had an end in mind, one that was good and peaceable. Praise God!

You see, we are predestined, even before we are born, to be conformed into the image of His Son, Jesus the Christ (Rom. 8:29). Christ Himself said that, "I give unto them eternal life; and they shall never perish, neither shall any man pluck them out of my hand" (John 10:28). What an assurance to know that the promise of salvation given by the Lord, by the grace of God, is irrevocable, and that nothing can snatch us who are predestined from Him. Our salvation is sealed in promise, by the Holy Spirit. Ephesians 1:4 also states, "As He hath chosen us in him before the foundation of the world, that we should be holy and without blame before him in love." God has promised to never leave us nor forsake us (Heb. 13:5), and that He would finish what He has begun in us (Phil. 1:6).

Cry: A Voice in the Wilderness

Chapter Fourteen:
The Day of Our Salvation

"But he was wounded for our transgressions, he was bruised for our iniquities: the chastisement of our peace was upon him; and with his stripes we are healed."
(Isaiah 53:5, KJV)

Isaiah was a prophet of God who, from the time King Uzziah died (740 B.C.), prophesied the coming of the Messiah, Jesus Christ. He was one of the few writing prophets of his time. He spoke of the need for Israel's faithfulness to God, proclaimed God's power over other gods, and God's promise of judgment of nations and the deliverance of God's people. All throughout the Old Testament the Lord God has proclaimed salvation and healing to Israel and His remnant. "And it shall come to pass, that whosoever shall call on the name of the LORD shall be delivered" (Joel 2:32). This is one of my favorite scriptures in the Bible. It says that whosoever -- and that means anyone and everyone, no one excluded -- if we call on His name, we shall be delivered! It does not matter if we are rich or poor, male or female, drug addict or sex addict, if we seek Him, we will be delivered! Jesus said that He comes for those who are in need of a physician, and that was me!

According to the Word of God, mankind was lost. I was lost, and in need of a Savior. No matter how the children of Israel tried they, as well as I, would always end up straying from God and breaking commandments. Although there was a temporary process set in place to cover sin, there was no permanent solution to the sin of mankind. God so longed to save His people, His creation. At first glance, we look at ourselves (at least I did), and see our state, our sinful state and all our failures. We do not see God's plan of salvation, its simplicity and completeness.   One of the greatest challenges is for man to discover his sinful state and recognize that he (this includes women) needs forgiveness. This is something that I have seen a great many people run from. No one likes to accept that they are sinners, and according to God's law and judgment are deserving of His wrath and eternal death. It is easier to just put on the mask and delusion of atheism or creating another god that suits our selfish desires and rebellion, than to admit that we are sinners and in need of a savior. Many would rather turn to false religions and ignore all the magnificent, wondrous, and scientific proof of the existence of an omnipotent Creator. Some would rather close their eyes to the historical proof of the Bible, ever immersing themselves in ignorant bliss and false gods.

Then there are those who are searching for truth; those who are thirsting for righteousness, freedom and fulfillment. They are longing for a relationship with God. They know that something is missing in their lives; that no matter how hard they try, they keep missing the prize. *"Where is this God?"* they wonder. *"Who is this man Jesus?"* Many are agnostic. Many once believed in God, heard about Jesus, or even knew Him, and yet somehow, they strayed. Many got lost in the sea of life's pressures and temptations. How would they find their way back?

In God's infinite wisdom and mercy, He sent Jesus. Jesus' ministry on Earth was to call the sinner to repentance, to heal the sick and get back what was lost. "The Spirit of the Lord is upon me, because he hath anointed me to preach the gospel to the poor; he hath sent me to heal the brokenhearted, to preach deliverance to the captives, and recovering of sight to the blind, to set at liberty them that are bruised" (Luke 4:18). He said, "If a man has an hundred sheep, and one of them be gone astray, doth he not leave the ninety and nine, and goeth into the mountains, and seeketh that which is gone astray?" (Matt. 18:12). I was lost, or gone astray, but glory to God -- He came and sought after me. Jesus, praying for the disciples, said, "Those that thou gavest me I have kept, and none of them is lost" (John 17:12).

So, we see God had a plan of escape for mankind, for our sinful state. That plan is Jesus the Christ. John the Baptist cries in the wilderness, as do I, "Make straight the way of the Lord!" And, "Behold the Lamb of God, which taketh away the sin of the world" (John 1:23, 29). God's plan for deliverance is found in Christ and Christ alone, for "If the Son therefore shall make you free, ye shall be free indeed" (John 8:36). For Jesus says, "Except a man be born again, he cannot see the kingdom of God" (John 3:3). "That which is born of flesh is flesh; and that which is born of the Spirit is spirit" (John 3:6).

John 3:16 states that, "For God so loved the world, that he gave his only begotten Son, that whosoever believeth in him should not perish, but have everlasting life." However, those who reject the truth of Christ are described in John 3:19 -- "This is the condemnation, that light is come into the world, and men loved darkness rather than light, because their deeds were evil." He goes on to state in verse 36 that the wrath of God is on those who do not believe on Him.

One of the hardest things to do as a minister of Christ is to help others see their fallen state and need for forgiveness while showing the love and mercy that God has for them and provision He gives in Christ. It seems that we tend to shut down, or the spiritual enemy comes and distorts, perverts or steals the word. My prayer and the promise of God is that those who call on Him shall be delivered as He said in His Word. Christ says in John 3, in verse 17, "For God sent not his Son into the world to condemn the world; but that the world through him might be saved." I must challenge you, if you have not surrendered your heart and your life to Jesus -- do it today. Call on Him for your salvation, healing, and your deliverance. He hears you and will answer you.

Because we are saved by faith in Christ (Rom. 10:9) we can have assurance of God's promises of deliverance and healing. Nothing separates us from the love of God that is in Christ Jesus (Rom. 8:35-39). And if we would grab hold of that, by faith in His word, we will make great strides toward true freedom.

The last thing I want to share with you is something that the Lord shared with me one night. I was in my bedroom, and in pain in my heart. At this moment, I had reached my wits end in self-pursuit of relationships. Although I was delivered from drugs, the Lord was still working in me on my desire to be loved by a man. I was praying and I began to cry, from my soul. The Spirit of the Lord came into the room, and I began to talk with Him, just as you would talk with a friend. I said in prayer, "I don't know what's wrong with me, and I hurt so much, what's wrong with me? Why do I keep putting myself in this same position?" I continued, "Remember when I was a little girl? You said that You wanted me, and loved me … and then my life fell apart." I wailed.

Then in a soothing voice the Lord said, "Look at my hands and my feet – I did this for you." I could see them in the Spirit, as He held them out. Then He said, "Look at my side – I did this to protect you." As I saw His side, I felt the pain. I knew the love He had for me. I cried for what He did for me, for my healing, and salvation. I felt such love that night; knowing that I, His beloved, was precious to Him and He loved me as no man could.

That was a defining moment for me. This was one of many events - but the most profound and personal experience that I have ever known. It is as if I was Thomas in the Gospel of John. Thomas did not believe that the Lord was resurrected. He needed to see it for himself. He could not go on someone's word, but had to be an eyewitness to the resurrected body of Christ. Jesus appeared before him and told him to touch the very scars that He showed to me, and then proclaimed, "Thomas, because thou hast seen me, thou hast believed: blessed are they that have not seen, and yet have believed" (John 20:29). The Lord proved to me and to Thomas that He is real. Now I know that my Beloved Jesus paid a dear price for my salvation and deliverance, and that price is one that no other man could ever have paid -- His life.

My prayer, beloved one, is that you be encouraged and know without a doubt that God loves you so dearly. If you would just look spiritually at His hands, His feet, His side, and His stripes; you would see that He did that for YOU! Accept His love and His healing today! It is yours and it has already been paid for! Know that there will be great rejoicing in the Heaven among the angels of God as you enter into the Kingdom of God. "It was meet that we should make merry, and be glad: for this thy brother was dead, and is alive again; and was lost, and is found" (Luke 15:32).

Repent and turn to your God! Ask for forgiveness and forgive others! Be baptized, pick up your cross and follow Him!

Part Seven:

Manifestation and Impartation

Chapter Fifteen:
Finished Work

"Being confident of this very thing, that he which hath begun a good work in
you will perform it until the day of Jesus Christ."
(Philippians 1:6, KJV)

Beloved ones, I praise God for you and for your diligence in seeking the mysteries of God in Christ. Again, I say that it is by a divine appointment that you have this book in your hand. I pray that my testimony of victory has served to witness to the power and dominion of Christ over ALL the power of the enemy and his cohorts!

Let me begin this chapter by stating that it is not a typographical error, nor is it an oversight, that the last part of this book is labeled "Part Seven," without regard for a "Part Six." Before the first edition printing of this book the Lord revealed to me, by the man of God Apostle Naim D. Collins, that I was to prophesy over this book and every reader of this work. I immediately received confirmation. As the Lord spoke to me, I inquired of what I believed to be a finished work, and wondered why He would add another chapter or part. It was vitally important to me that the symmetry and prophetic message contained in this book not be changed, for I know that the hand of the Lord is upon this work for the express purpose of destroying the works of the devil.

The Lord showed me that this book had not in fact been completed. Up until this day this book expresses the grace of God that leads to total deliverance and hope for salvation. This book exemplifies the power of Christ and His resurrection in the life of a believer, whosoever will believe. However, the Lord's will is to take you beyond merely experiencing second hand the grace given by Him in the person of Jesus Christ -- to a tangible experience in which you will be totally transformed by His presence!

The number seven represents a complete work. It speaks of the completed work and victory of the Cross at Calvary, where victory was taken and the fate of satan sealed. Revelation 12:11 states: "And they overcame him by the blood of the Lamb, and by the word of their testimony." This is the testimony of my victory obtained by that very blood that was shed on Calvary. As Yeshua (Jesus) died on the cross, He proclaimed, "It is finished." Yes beloved, the work is finished, the price was paid, and the judgment has been set against the evil one himself. He is the one who has already been judged. Salvation is not offered or given to satan, but to you!

Conversely, the number six represents the number of man. When one receives the gift of life given through the crucifixion and resurrection of Christ Jesus, the Son of God, the old things are in fact passed away and all things are made new (2 Cor. 5:17). This means the old man (human nature) with its sin nature has in fact been crucified with Christ, and no longer exists. In Heaven, there is no account of the old person, the slate has been wiped clean (Heb. 10:17). Therefore, there is no record in the Heaven of your sin, once you are born again. There is no record of the number of man – six. In fact, there is only the new completed man, the resurrected man represented by the complete work of Christ, for the old man has been crucified (Gal. 2:20).

Chapter Sixteen:
Apostolic Impartation

"Thou shalt also decree a thing, and it shall be established unto thee: and the
light shall shine upon thy ways."
(Job 22:28, KJV)

As an Apostolic-prophetic voice to the nations, ordained and
appointed by God Himself, through the grace and power given unto me by
the blood of the Lamb of God (Jesus) and His Holy Spirit, I decree and
declare the following:

Cry: A Voice in the Wilderness, is the prophetic voice of one crying in
the wilderness. It represents every spiritual cry that has or will ever go out
unto the Father in Heaven from His children who are caught under the
demonic, satanic, and wicked bonds and plans of the enemy. For every voice
that has cried out for deliverance and relief from the bonds of tyranny that
the enemy has placed on them, *Cry: A Voice in the Wilderness,* serves as the
apostolic and prophetic power of God in the Earth to judge the evil works of
the enemy, and to bring salvation and deliverance to the remnant people of
God. *Cry* serves as the sword of God to annihilate the wickedness and
perversion that the enemy has wrought on the Earth, and to manifest the
Kingdom of God and of His Christ!

I declare in the name of Jesus Christ (Yeshua ha Meshiach) that you,
the reader, shall not be the same! I pray for a release of fresh oil and fire of
God in your life that would shake your very foundation and thrust you into

the Kingdom of God and Christ Jesus! I say that today, by the hearing of the gospel of the Kingdom and of our Lord, you shall be made free! For the Word of God says that you shall know the truth and the truth shall make you free (John 8:32)! I prophetically proclaim that every person that reads this book that is under the oppression of the enemy in any way shall be free! I release the holy angels of the Lord God to minister to every person reading, that your deliverance and salvation be made manifest in the life of this reader! I pray a covering of the Holy Spirit around this reader and pray for a release in the spirit realm of the healing that is needed! I command every wicked and foul spirit and power to be broken by the power of the blood of Yeshua, and command them to go to the desolate places! I pray that the reader's steps now be ordered by the Lord without hindrance to the place of refuge that is needed! I call forth great intercessors and ministers to be brought into the life of this reader to minister complete deliverance and wholeness to the entire person (spirit, soul, mind and body) in the name of Yeshua!

I say that you, reader, are predestined and ordained by God to be conformed into the image of His Son Jesus (Yeshua ha Meshiach)! And that He who has begun a good work in you shall complete it (Rom. 8:29; Phil. 1:6)! Amen, so be it!

If you have not already done so, please take the time right now to accept the gift of eternal life. It is free. Romans 10:9 states: "That if thou shalt confess with thy mouth the Lord Jesus, and shalt believe in thine heart that God hath raised him from the dead, thou shalt be saved." Take the time, beloved, to receive Christ today. He accepts you as you are. He came and died for you - the lost one and the sinner.

If you have given your life to the Lord already, no matter how long ago it was or maybe just yesterday, and you know in your heart that you have not allowed Him to be "Lord" over your life; then repent today and ask for forgiveness, for I John 1:9 says: "If we confess our sins, he is faithful and just to forgive us our sins, and to cleanse us from all unrighteousness."

Pray this simple sincere prayer now:

"Lord God, I realize that I have sinned against You - that I am a sinner and rightfully under the law of sin and death. But today I repent, turn away from my sin and rebellion, and ask that You please forgive me and cleanse me from all unrighteousness. I believe that Jesus is Your Son and that He came in the flesh and died for my sins, and that You raised Him from the dead. Jesus, I ask that You come into my heart and be my Lord, and reveal Your Kingdom to me. Jesus, I thank You for saving me now and I openly confess that You are my perfect Lord and Savior. Amen!"

Welcome – sisters and brothers -- into the Body of Christ and into the Kingdom of God!!! Remember, the Kingdom is not of this world, but seek the LORD and you shall find it.

"For the kingdom of God is not meat and drink; but righteousness, and peace, and joy in the Holy Ghost" (Rom. 14:17). "For the kingdom of God is not in word, but in power" (I Cor. 4:20). "And I say unto you, Ask, and it shall be given you; seek, and ye shall find; knock, and it shall be opened unto you" (Luke 11:9).

Seek the Lord this day, beloved ones, while He may be found, and

He will answer you, heal you, and establish you in His righteousness. "He shall call upon me, and I will answer him: I will be with him in trouble; I will deliver him, and honour him. With long life will I satisfy him, and shew him my salvation" (Psalm 91:15-16). Amen!

<u>READER'S NOTES</u>

- 113 -

<u>READER'S NOTES</u>

- 114 -